ISRAEL
and the Neighboring Arab States

Scale of Miles

MEDITERRANEAN

SEA

LEBANON

SYRIA

Rosh Hanikra

Hulieh Marshes

Mishmar Hayarden

GALILEE

Sea of Galilee

Haifa

Tiberias

Nazareth

JORDAN

Tel Aviv

Sarona

Jaffa

Hakirya

Kibya

Amman

Lydda (Lod)

Jericho

Jerusalem

Shuneh

Deir Yassin

Bethlehem

Kfar Etzion

Gaza STRIP

Beersheba

Bir Ashu

El Auja (Nitzana)

NEGEV

EGYPT

Cairo

Suez Canal

SINAI

Eilat

Aqaba

Gulf of Suez

Gulf of Aqaba

SAUDI

ARABIA

Sharm Esh-Sheikh

RED SEA

Nile River

THE

FIRST TEN YEARS

A Diplomatic History of Israel

WALTER EYTAN

SIMON AND SCHUSTER

NEW YORK

1958

LIBRARY OF CONGRESS CATALOG CARD NUMBER: 58-9039

MANUFACTURED IN THE UNITED STATES OF AMERICA
BY AMERICAN BOOK—STRATFORD PRESS, INC., NEW YORK

Foreword

ISRAEL HAS HAD *a very full ten years. It is impossible in a book of this scope to deal in detail with even one aspect of them, that of external relations. But it should be possible to give a general idea of the problems that have faced us in this field, and this is what I have tried to do. This is no work of political science; there is little in it of theory or speculation. It is a narrative account of some of the chief matters that have arisen in the conduct of Israel's foreign policy, subjective and necessarily incomplete. I hope it may be of use or interest as an outline of Israel's early history.*

I have been able to draw on the memory of my colleagues where my own has failed, and on the research and reference services of my Ministry. I owe thanks to all who have helped me with facts, figures and judgments, but the responsibility for what this book contains is wholly mine. Nothing I have put into it can in any way bind or commit the Israel Government.

W. E.

JERUSALEM, SEPTEMBER 20, 1957

Contents

Maps

Illustrations

ix

THE
FIRST TEN YEARS

I

The First Year

ISRAEL WAS BORN in circumstances which were truly unique. For two thousand years the revival of the Jewish state in Palestine had been the passion and dream of a scattered people. For fifty years it had been a political program—and for the last five, at least, a certainty. Toward the end of 1947 it became a recommendation of the United Nations General Assembly.

If this Jewish state came into being six months later, it was not primarily because the United Nations had recommended it. That half-year had been enough for the General Assembly to take fright, as it was often to do later, at Arab violence and threats. It had begun to wobble and think of changing its mind. When the day of independence dawned, the decision was Israel's alone. The courage to take it grew from the stored-up anguish of those two thousand years. The debate which was still going on in the United Nations might have been a metaphysical disputation for all the effect it had on the events at Tel Aviv.

It was May 1948. Moshe Sharett started work as Foreign Minister of Israel by sending cables to other governments, informing them of the establishment of the new state and asking them to recognize it. He had a secretary and a personal assistant—that was all. Israel's independence had been proclaimed only a few hours before. As the messages flashed out to Paris and Rome, to Monrovia, Tegucigalpa and Bangkok, to the capitals of almost all the countries in the world, the armies of five Arab states converged on Israel and crossed her borders. There were air-raid alarms and sniping, gunfire in the distance. No one knew what the morrow or the next hour might bring.

In New York the General Assembly of the United Nations was breaking up in confusion, its metaphysics overtaken by events. The staff on which Mr. Sharett had counted as the nucleus of his Ministry was shut off in Jerusalem, beleaguered. Everything was new, everything makeshift. A gazetteer was called for to check the spelling of the more difficult capitals. Reykjavik, we were told later, was one. There was a hammering and a shifting of furniture as the farmsteads of Sarona, near Tel Aviv, formerly a German Templars' village, were turned into offices for the Provisional Government of Israel.

That day saw the culmination of a political struggle without parallel. It had started with the publication of Herzl's *The State of the Jews* in 1896 and the first Zionist Congress in 1897. There followed the Balfour Declaration in 1917 and nearly thirty years of the British mandatory rule which had ended, more ingloriously than it need have, the night before. It was a year to the day since the General Assembly set up the committee which had recommended the establishment of Israel, the Jewish state.

Events had moved fast. In 1946 the British Foreign Secretary had promised the Anglo-American Committee of Inquiry that he would implement their report if it was unanimous. The Committee presented a unanimous report, but Britain had not accepted it, despite Mr. Bevin's promise. A Labor Government was faced with the alternative of continuing to rule Palestine with ever more oppressive force, inviting ever more desperate violence and resistance, under a League of Nations mandate whose validity had been undermined with the League's disappearance, or of referring the whole problem to the United Nations, which had taken the League's place as the supreme international organization.

The United Nations, in its salad days, had acted with self-confidence and dispatch. The Secretary-General summoned a special session of the General Assembly, which met in April 1947. After a businesslike debate which lasted only two weeks, the Assembly on May 15 set up a Special Committee, which was to "submit such proposals as it may consider appropriate for the solution of the problem of Palestine." The report was to be communicated to the Secretary-General not later than September 1 so that it could be circulated to the members of the United Nations in time for consideration by the General Assembly that autumn.

UNSCOP—the United Nations Special Committee on Palestine—discharged its task with energy. Consisting of the representatives of Australia, Canada, Czechoslovakia, Guatemala, India, Iran, the Netherlands, Peru, Sweden, Uruguay and Yugoslavia, it completed its report punctually on September 1. It recommended, by a decisive majority, the partition of Palestine and its division between two new independent states, a Jewish and an Arab, to be linked in economic union. Jerusalem was to be a *corpus separatum* under international administration.

UNSCOP's plan was reminiscent of that which the Royal Commission, under the chairmanship of Lord Peel, had recommended ten years before. The 1937 plan had been accepted, despite misgivings, by the Jewish Agency for Palestine. The Arabs had rejected it because they could not tolerate the idea of a Jewish state in even part of Palestine. The British Government had first accepted it but a few months later changed its mind. Despite the great war which had shaken the world during most of the years between 1937 and 1947, the logic of the Palestine situation remained unchanged. UNSCOP arrived at substantially the same conclusions as the Royal Commission of a decade before. Again, the Jewish Agency accepted them—despite misgivings, mainly about Jerusalem. Again the Arabs rejected them outright, unwilling to reconcile themselves to anything short of Arab rule over the whole of Palestine. Great Britain, having left the problem at the door of the United Nations, could not actively oppose UNSCOP's proposals, but she made it clear that she would not co-operate in their implementation. She did not like the idea of a Jewish state.

UNSCOP's plan was remarkable for its territorial provisions. It divided Palestine into seven sections. Three of them were to form the Jewish state and three the Arab. Jerusalem was the seventh, an enclave within the Arab state. The six sections were arranged jigsaw-fashion, roughly following the demographic composition of the country. The whole was held together by two "kissing points," at each of which two sections of the Jewish state and two of the Arab met. In this way it would be possible to move freely throughout the Jewish state without ever touching Arab territory, and the Arabs could likewise move freely throughout their state without ever having to set foot in the Jewish. Jews traveling to Jerusalem would have to cross through the Arab state. It was the weirdest map ever drawn, a testimonial to the perplexity, sincerity and ingenuity of its authors. The Jewish state was to have some 55 per cent of the total area of Palestine, leaving 45 per cent to the Arabs. This division was not so inequitable as it sounds, since over half the Jewish state was to consist of the Negev, an uncultivated and largely uncultivable desert. In terms of arable land, the Arabs received at least their fair share.

This plan was endorsed, with slight modifications, by the General Assembly. The debate which for over two months raged at Lake Success was bitter, unsentimental, fierce. Everyone sensed a historic responsibility. When the vote was taken on November 29, 1947, thirty-three members voted for the resolution, with thirteen against and ten abstaining. This was more than the required two-thirds majority. On paper, the Jewish state was born. Of the thirteen states which opposed its creation, six were Arab, four more were Moslem. The others were Cuba, Greece and India. The United States and the Soviet Union supported the resolution; Great Britain abstained.

The General Assembly's decision was received with unbounded enthusiasm by the Jews of Palestine and by Jews throughout the world, with dismay by the Arabs and their friends. The Jewish Agency, in welcoming the decision, held out the hand of friendship to the Arabs. But trouble started the very next day. An Arab gang ambushed traffic near Tel Aviv. Seven Jews were killed.

If events had moved fast in 1947, in 1948 they were to move faster still. The General Assembly's resolution had been drafted and passed on the assumption that it could be carried into effect peacefully with the co-operation of all concerned. The British mandate for Palestine was to "terminate as soon as possible but in any case not later than 1 August 1948." British forces were to be withdrawn "progressively," the with-

5

drawal to be completed also "as soon as possible but in any case not later than 1 August 1948." The Arab and Jewish states were to come into existence "two months after the evacuation of the armed forces of the mandatory Power has been completed but in any case not later than 1 August 1948." Britain at that time maintained 100,000 troops in Palestine— an index of the country's disturbed state and of the British belief that this sort of disturbance could be checked by force.

Matters were to turn out differently. Arab attacks were intensified, and all Palestine was soon in turmoil. Armed gangs were sent in by the neighboring Arab states, with a stiffening of officers and N.C.O.s from their regular armies. Long before the British mandate ended, at a time when Britain was still "responsible for law and order," * Syrian bands were operating in Palestine. An "Arab Liberation Army" was fighting up and down the country, with arms (up to medium tanks) from Lebanon and Transjordan. An Iraqi officer was in command of Arab forces in Jaffa, the twin of Tel Aviv. It was not possible to travel from Jerusalem to the coast except in convoy, with armed escort; after some weeks it became impossible to travel at all. Jerusalem was surrounded by a large Arab force and besieged. Britain announced May 15 as the date for the termination of her mandate. The withdrawal of her armed forces was to be completed later. (Sir Alan Cunningham, the High Commissioner, sailed from Haifa on May 14, symbolizing the end of British rule. The last British troops embarked on June 30.)

Not since the Crusades had Jerusalem been besieged for so long as it was in 1948. A convoy fought its way through at Easter, but thereafter, under sustained sniping and artillery shelling, the Jewish population of the city was cut off from the rest of the country. There was no food, no tap water, no petrol,

---

* Mr. A. Creech Jones, Secretary of State for the Colonies, in the House of Commons, December 11, 1947.

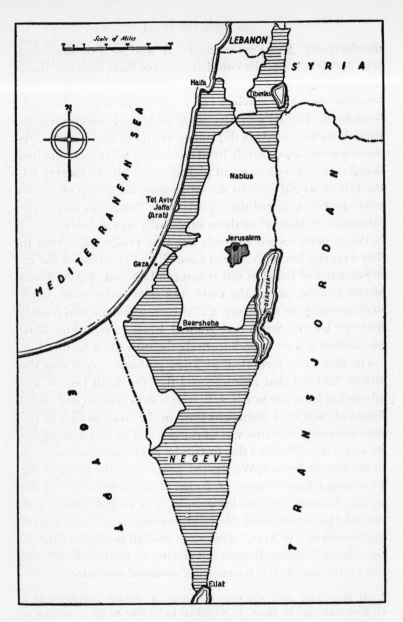

The Partition Boundaries (1947)

no electricity. Shops were empty. It was the first time that Jewish Agency officials could subsist on their salaries; there was nothing to spend them on. Water from cisterns was brought round by carriers every other day, a pail for each household. The lack of electricity produced unexpected results. Wireless receivers did not work; there was no news. As there was no news, people lived on rumor: what someone had heard that someone else had picked up on his old battery set, the tale of an old man in the synagogue, the gossip of housewives as they searched their gardens for dandelion leaves, the "situation estimates" of those supposedly in the know.

When news seeped through late that Friday night that in Tel Aviv the Jewish National Council had proclaimed the independence of Israel, it was at first not believed. Tel Aviv was at the farthest end of the earth, not forty miles away. Early next morning, in the street, a CBS correspondent told friends that the United States had granted Israel recognition. How one wished it were true, but surely the man was a babbler!

On May 14 in Jerusalem we knew nothing, except that the British had left that morning and that the Arab Legion was advancing from the north. A British consul general had established himself near Damascus Gate in the Arab section of the city. His telephone line was working,* and he was making his presence felt. Within a day or two he began sending messages to the Jewish Agency. We replied, proudly, in the name of the Provisional Government of Israel. This game went on for weeks. Another went on for months. The British consul general at Haifa addressed his communications to "the Jewish authorities at Tel Aviv." This was a studied insult, on instructions from London, Britain not having recognized Israel and her Government. His letters were returned unopened.

---

* It is working still, the only telephone in Jordan connected to a civilian exchange in Israel. It is curious to be able to get a number in enemy territory simply by dialing it.

sending of the letter as such was a tribute to his own quick thinking and action. President Truman reacted as quickly; he tells the story in his book.* The White House announcement ran:

> This Government has been informed that a Jewish state has been proclaimed in Palestine and recognition has been requested by the Provisional Government thereof. The United States recognizes the Provisional Government as the *de facto* authority of the new State of Israel.

The American delegation at the General Assembly, arguing at that time in favor of trusteeship for Palestine, was taken completely by surprise. So was the Assembly as a whole. So was Israel. To be recognized so swiftly by the United States was a near-miracle, certainly the greatest thing that could have happened at that moment to the infant state, on the eve of invasion by enemies sworn to strangle it at birth.

The full extent of America's recognition of Israel became apparent later. Mr. Philip Jessup, the United States delegate, speaking on December 17, 1948, in the Security Council on the admission of Israel to membership in the United Nations, explained it:

> . . . the United States extended immediate and full recognition of the State of Israel. Perhaps some confusion arises between recognition of the State of Israel and recognition of the Provisional Government of Israel. So far as recognition of the

---

* Harry S Truman, *Years of Trial and Hope* (New York, Doubleday and Company, Inc., 1956), p. 164. Mr. Truman writes that the announcement was handed to the press "exactly eleven minutes after Israel had been proclaimed a state." He must mean eleven minutes after independence came into effect at midnight (Israel time) on May 14-15. The proclamation had been made eight hours earlier.

State of Israel is concerned . . . the recognition accorded by the United States Government to the State of Israel was immediate and full recognition. There was no qualification. It was not conditional; it was not *de facto* recognition; it was full recognition. So far as the Provisional Government of Israel is concerned, the United States did extend *de facto* recognition to that Provisional Government of Israel.

Elections were held in Israel on January 25, 1949. Six days later the United States announced its *de jure* recognition of the Government of Israel.

The second country to recognize Israel was Guatemala, on May 15,* and the third the Soviet Union, on May 18. Within a few days, five Eastern European countries and five Latin American had followed suit. But by the beginning of August no more than fifteen countries had recognized Israel. Apart from one or two additions, the list remained static until after the turn of the year, when a large number of countries recognized Israel or her Government, or both. Those included France, Great Britain, most of the countries of Western Europe, members of the British Commonwealth, and more Latin American states. By February 1, 1949, the number of countries recognizing Israel had grown to thirty-three. This figure corresponded exactly to the number of countries which had voted in the General Assembly for Israel's independence, but, including as it did several countries which were not members of the United Nations, it meant that even now not all the countries which had voted aye on November 29, 1947, were prepared to carry their vote to its logical conclusion and recognize

---

* Announced by the Foreign Minister in a cable dated May 17. The delegate of Guatemala on UNSCOP, Licenciado Jorge Garcia Granados, had been a protagonist of partition and had taken a prominent part in the General Assembly debate. In 1955 he became Guatemala's first Minister to Israel.

the new state. By March 1, 1949, the figure had risen to forty-five, by early April to fifty-three. By then the battle for recognition had been won; the final act was to come in the following month with Israel's election to membership in the United Nations.

Recognition of Israel was accompanied by so many complications, and it led other countries to follow such varying procedures, that it has become a classic of international law. But despite the legal nature of the act of recognition, in no case does the decision to recognize or not to recognize seem to have been based on law alone. Political rather than legal considerations proved decisive, though legal difficulties were sometimes pleaded—for instance, by Great Britain—as an excuse for not granting recognition or not granting it in a certain form.

Where a distinction was made between recognition *de facto* and *de jure,* the former in most cases was followed by the latter. Some countries granted *de jure* recognition after the elections of January 25, 1949, whether or not they had recognized Israel *de facto* before. Switzerland stated that her *de facto* recognition had been no more than a figure of speech, and that she had intended *de jure* recognition from the start. Canada, which had recognized Israel *de facto* on November 24, 1948, interpreted her vote for Israel's admission to the United Nations as implicit recognition *de jure* and did not think it necessary to make any further announcement on the subject. South Africa, which had insisted * that her *de facto* recognition of May 24, 1948, was to be interpreted strictly as *de facto* only, found it necessary to announce *de jure* recognition, on

---

* On September 22, 1948, Israel notified South Africa that she wished to appoint a visa officer at Johannesburg. Over four months later, on January 28, 1949, "after careful consideration . . . and study of possible implications," the Union Government agreed, "on the understanding, however, that such assent should not be construed as *de jure* recognition of Israel."

the same occasion, explicitly: "I have pleasure in informing you," her Prime Minister cabled on May 14, 1949, "that with the admission of Israel to the United Nations the Government of the Union of South Africa accord *de jure* recognition to the State of Israel." Ireland recognized Israel *de facto* on February 12, 1949. The fact that her delegation, by the chance of alphabetical order, sits next to that of Israel at the United Nations has made no difference. Ireland, for some Irish reason, to this day does not recognize Israel *de jure*. The pattern is infinitely varied.

In international law, a state, to be recognized as such, is supposed to have clearly defined boundaries. This was not the case with Israel, or so, at least, it could be argued. On this point, the attitude of other countries varied as much as it did on *de facto* and *de jure* recognition. Most made no reference to the question at all. They recognized Israel without alluding to her frontiers, unaware, or preferring to act as if they were unaware, that these still constituted a problem. But in some cases the frontiers were in the center of the picture. South Africa, in according *de facto* recognition, made a reservation:

> In view of the resolution of the United Nations General Assembly of 29 November 1947, which is based on partition, this recognition is not in respect of any particular boundaries, and the Union Government will be prepared to accord similar recognition to an Arab area in Palestine either as a separate state or as incorporated into neighbouring Arab states.

When France recognized the Provisional Government of Israel *de facto* on January 24, 1949, she stipulated that "this decision does not prejudge the definitive delimitation by the United Nations of the territory on which it will exercise its authority." Turkey, two months later, adopted the same attitude: her recognition was not to "prejudge the question of the delimitation of the frontiers of the new state." The Prime Minister of New Zealand, informing Israel of *de facto* recognition on January 29, 1949, cabled: "It is the understanding of the New Zealand Government that the settlement of boundaries and other outstanding questions will be effected in accordance with the resolution of the General Assembly of the United Nations of 11 December 1948."

Israel had always taken it for granted that she would join the United Nations. The General Assembly itself had, indeed, stated in its resolution of November 29, 1947, that when the independence of "either the Arab or the Jewish State" had become effective, "sympathetic consideration should be given to its application for admission to membership in the United Nations." This made it clear that Israel's admission was to be considered on its own merits and could not be made dependent on whether the Arab state applied too or, indeed, came into existence at all. But apart altogether from the General Assembly's desire that Israel's admission to the United Nations should be sympathetically considered, Israel herself strongly desired admission, both because this would set the seal of international recognition on her independent statehood, and because her own ideals of brotherhood and peace demanded it. Membership in the United Nations was regarded as the highest good; it was seen less as a right than as a privilege and an aspiration.

When Israel submitted her application—symbolically, on November 29, 1948—she had been recognized by only nineteen other countries. The Security Council had called for an armistice to be negotiated between her and the Arab states.

It was a season of uneasy truce; by the time Israel's application was considered in the Security Council, fighting had again broken out. Syria, at that time a member of the Security Council, bitterly opposed the proposal in the name of all the Arab states. Despite the support of the United States and the Soviet

Union, only five members of the Security Council voted in favor. Five abstained, and one, Syria, voted against. The application accordingly failed.

It was debated again early in the following year. By this time the fighting had ended, and the first of the armistice agreements had been signed. Elections had been held; the Provisional Government had given way to a Government constituted on the basis of the election results. The countries recognizing Israel now included forty-five out of the fifty-eight members of the United Nations. The prospects, if not cast-iron, were much better than they had been a few months before. On February 24, 1949, the day she signed the armistice agreement with Egypt, Israel asked the Security Council to give renewed consideration to her request. On March 4, with only Egypt voting against, and Great Britain abstaining, the Security Council recommended Israel's admission to membership. On May 11, the General Assembly accepted the recommendation and decided to admit Israel as a member of the United Nations. The countries which opposed it were the six Arab states, together with Afghanistan, India, Iran and Pakistan, all of which had voted against the establishment of Israel in the first place, Burma, which at the time of the 1947 vote was herself not yet a member of the United Nations, and Ethiopia, assuring herself of Arab support on Eritrea.*

---

* The list of abstainers was more varied: Belgium, Brazil and El Salvador, Catholic countries which knew that Israel could not reconcile herself to the internationalization of Jerusalem; Sweden, supported by Denmark, in protest against the unsolved murder of Count Bernadotte; Greece, to preserve from harm the large Hellenic colony in Egypt; Turkey, for Moslem solidarity; Thailand, unwilling to oppose the rest of Asia; and Great Britain, still sulking. Turkey's abstention did nothing to increase Israel's confidence in her as a member of the Conciliation Commission, then sitting in conference at Lausanne. The variety of the grounds for abstention and of course opposition showed how warily Israel had to move in her international relations.

Israel's election to membership in the United Nations came exactly a year, almost to the day, after the proclamation of her independence. It was hailed as a historic and joyous event, second only to the attainment of statehood itself. "By our admission to the United Nations," Mr. Sharett told the Knesset on June 15, "the highest seal has been placed on our international recognition." It was more than a major political occurrence; it was a deeply moving human event. It brought Israel back into the community of nations. It conferred on the Jewish people equal rights with all free nations. It closed the dark chapter of persecution, degradation and discrimination. It seemed difficult, he said, to gauge the full import of that revolutionary change: "a new and complex responsibility has devolved upon us." *

In the meantime, the Foreign Ministry had been preoccupied with other problems, no less pressing.

On May 14, 1948, everything seemed to be happening at once. This had, indeed, been a feature of the situation for some months. Not all the things that were happening at the same time were compatible with one another. The General Assembly had, under the partition resolution, set up a commission to take over the administration of Palestine "progressively," as the mandatory Power withdrew its armed forces, and to establish provisional councils of government in the Jewish and Arab states. This commission, known as the Palestine Commission (*not* the later Palestine Conciliation Commission), consisted of Bolivia, Czechoslovakia, Denmark, Panama and the Philippines. The Assembly asked that the mandatory Power "to the fullest possible extent co-ordinate its plans for

---

* For an interesting account of Israel's admission to UN membership, see *Israel and the United Nations*, National Studies on International Organization (New York, Carnegie Endowment for International Peace, 1956), pp. 49–61.

withdrawal with the plans of the Commission to take over and administer areas which have been evacuated." The mandatory Power did nothing of the kind. It was determined not to co-operate in implementing partition, though at what exact moment it decided to leave Palestine without handing over authority to anyone—the policy that came to be known as Operation Chaos—is not known. "The mandatory Power," the resolution had gone on to say, "shall not take any action to prevent, obstruct or delay the implementation by the Commission of the measures recommended by the General Assembly." Yet this is precisely what the mandatory Power did. It refused to allow the Palestine Commission to come to Palestine at all. The most the Commission could do was to send an advance party of officials led by Pablo de Azcárate, who had been the Spanish Republic's Ambassador to the Court of St. James's and was later to serve as General Secretary of the Conciliation Commission. Its other members were an Indian economist, a Greek lawyer and a Norwegian colonel, assisted by two women secretaries.

The Palestine Government did all it could to show this strangely assorted group that it was not welcome. The six of them were housed in an unventilated basement opposite British military headquarters in Jerusalem, where they did their courageous best to represent the might and majesty of the United Nations. Under indescribable conditions they tried to work and arrange to take over the administration of Palestine. But as the secretaries were kept busy housekeeping, and the men were forced to go foraging for food and drink, they would have found the task beyond them even if the mandatory Power had been in a mood to co-operate. As it was, when May 14 came and the General Assembly, having appointed a Mediator, relieved the Palestine Commission "from the further exercise of its responsibilities," Señor de Azcárate and his quintet had through no fault of their own achieved nothing. Unable to make their way out of the beleaguered city, they stayed on to share the hardships of the siege with the Jewish population, glad to be spared the humiliations to which the mandatory Power had subjected them.

The General Assembly on that same May 14 was discussing an American proposal that Palestine be put temporarily under trusteeship. When it was seen that Arab opposition and British non-co-operation left the partition resolution little chance of peaceful implementation, the Security Council, on April 1, had asked the Secretary-General to convoke a special session of the General Assembly "to consider further the question of the future Government of Palestine." Here was the first surrender to Arab violence. Instead of insisting that all concerned respect the resolution it had adopted after exhaustive debate only four months before, the General Assembly began to beat a strategic, certainly a tactical, retreat. The trusteeship proposal showed the way. It was as far as could be from the realities of the struggle in Palestine. The discussion was in full swing when a message was received that Israel had proclaimed her independence, followed shortly by the announcement of America's recognition. The *volte-face* was complete.

There was nothing more the General Assembly could do or say. Events had betrayed the unreality of its thinking. The President of the Assembly, in a closing speech, said the people of Palestine would decide their future for themselves. Freedom never came as a gift; it had to be conquered, often at the price of tears and suffering. The Assembly must hope that the fratricidal struggle in Palestine would cease as soon as possible. It must greet the advent of a new free people to the concert of nations and hope that the peoples of Palestine, whatever their race and origin, would realize that their immediate interests and their future depended on mutual understanding without foreign intervention.

These were brave words, adapted to a difficult situation.

Four months were to pass before the General Assembly again occupied itself with the Palestine question. By then most of the fighting was over, the Arab invasion repelled and Israel firmly established.

Where the General Assembly left off, the Security Council took over. The Council had, as it was, been occupying itself with the situation in Palestine for the greater part of the year. On March 5 it had called for consultations between its permanent members (the "Great Powers") and appealed "to all Governments and peoples, particularly in and around Palestine, to take all possible action to prevent or reduce such disorders as are now occurring in Palestine." By April 1 its language had become more peremptory. It called upon "Arab and Jewish armed groups in Palestine to cease acts of violence immediately" and asked the two sides "to make representatives available to the Security Council for the purpose of arranging a truce," emphasizing "the heavy responsibility which would fall upon any party failing to observe such a truce."

All this was of no avail. Arab irregulars continued to stream into Palestine from the neighboring countries. In most parts of Palestine the mandatory Power had long ceased to exercise authority, but the Security Council seemed not to know this. In a new resolution on April 17 it called for a cessation of "all activities of a military or para-military nature" and asked all persons and organizations in Palestine to "co-operate with the Mandatory authorities for the effective maintenance of law and order." Considering "the United Kingdom Government . . . responsible for the maintenance of peace and order in Palestine," the Council requested it "to use its best efforts to bring all those concerned . . . to accept the measures" proposed in the resolution. The resolution struck only one note of realism, or accurate appraisal, when it called upon "all Governments and particularly those of the countries neighboring Palestine to take all possible steps to assist in the implementation of the measures . . . particularly those referring to the entry into Palestine of armed bands and fighting personnel, groups and individuals and weapons and war materials." Here at least was recognition of the fact that fighting men were streaming into Palestine from all the Arab countries around. But it was of course disingenuous to expect the governments of these countries to dam the stream when they were obviously doing all in their power to reinforce it.

This resolution, as anyone in Palestine could have told the Council in advance, was to be of no more effect than those that went before. In its last action before May 14, the Council established a Truce Commission "composed of representatives of those members of the Security Council which have career consular officers in Jerusalem." This meant the United States, France and Belgium. It was a neat way of keeping out the Soviet Union, which had no consul in Jerusalem, and other Communist countries, which, though represented there, were not members of the Security Council. The function of the Commission, appointed on April 23, was to assist the Council in "supervising the implementation by the parties of the resolution of 17 April." The commission operated, or tried to operate, under unbelievably difficult conditions. The American consul general was killed by an Arab sniper's bullet on his way home from one of its meetings. Here is a contemporary account of the commission's meeting on the morning of May 14, two hours after the British pulled out of Jerusalem, and six hours before the independence of Israel was proclaimed at Tel Aviv:

The atmosphere at the French Consulate was nervous and tense. The Truce Commission was in session. The presence of a Belgian, a Frenchman, an American, a Norwegian and a Spaniard symbolized the United Nations. Every few minutes the telephone rang—to pass some piece of news, to tell the Belgian consul about the fate of his wounded driver, to bring messages from the Arabs, to announce that the Polish consul had disappeared. But it was not only this that made the quiet conduct of negotiations impossible. Bullets were whizzing past or hitting the building all the time. Suddenly a Red Cross man came in panting with the latest news from Kfar Etzion. Repeated efforts were made to arrange a cease-fire for the Arab representatives, who claimed they were unable to reach the Consulate because of the heavy fighting. Meanwhile an aged manservant went round offering arak. The Belgian consul kept twittering, the Frenchman jumped up and down nervily. The American looked solemn . . . while the Spaniard maintained a posture of prayer and contemplation. When accusations of bad faith started flying like bullets, while it was clear that nothing effective was being done, there was nothing for it but to go. It was like a nightmare, and the drive back was not much better.*

The French consul general, a distinguished archaeologist of eccentric ways, was furious with Señor de Azcárate for keeping so calm. Pointing at him, he cried in disgust: "That man—he calls himself a Spaniard!" It was an exciting time, and everyone, certainly if he had Latin blood in his veins, should be decently excited. The account continues:

The work of the Truce Commission has been made difficult by a number of circumstances. The Arabs have been reluctant to meet them, and have found all sorts of excuses for putting them off. There is considerable rivalry and ill-feeling between the Commission and the Red Cross, which has proposals and ambitions of its own. On the Commission itself there is something of a split between the American and the other two members. At least as long as the British were here, the American

---

* This extract and the next are taken from a longer report, reproduced *in extenso* by Arthur Koestler in *Promise and Fulfilment* (London, 1949), pp. 234–38.

was closer to their point of view than his two colleagues. To add to the Commission's difficulties, communications between them and Lake Success are rather precarious, depending as they do on the vagaries of the American consul's radio tele-type. In consequence partly of these difficulties, but mostly of the difficulties inherent in the situation itself, the Truce Commission has so far achieved nothing. It is true, however, at least of the French and Belgian members, and certainly of the Spanish and Norwegian members of the U.N. staff, that they would be happy to achieve something if they only knew how.

The Truce Commission, composed as it was of three consular officers in Jerusalem, was cut off from the rest of the country. It was subsequently referred to by the Security Council as "the Truce Commission for Palestine," but it never operated outside Jerusalem. Even in Jerusalem it achieved nothing. It could never have been expected to achieve anything, had the Security Council understood what was happening in Palestine. How could three consuls stand between Jew and Arab at this climacteric moment in their history? It is not clear when, if at all, the Truce Commission was formally wound up. It appears to have faded away. It was referred to in a resolution of the Security Council as late as October 19, 1948, but even the Council must by that time have ceased to believe in its efficacy as an instrument of pacification. On the local scene it produced a last flicker of life on November 30, when a "United Nations Cease-Fire Agreement," concluded between the Arab and Israel commanders in the Jerusalem area "at the invitation of the United Nations Observers and the Security Council Truce Commission," was countersigned by a French consul.

The end of the mandate and the establishment of Israel on May 14 produced an immediate change in the fighting. Until

then there had been large-scale guerrilla activity by Arab irregulars; now war began in earnest. The regular armies of the
neighboring states had been held poised in reserve and now
crossed the frontiers. Israel had to fight for her life from the
moment she was born. The Security Council tried repeatedly
to impose a truce, but in vain. On May 22 it called upon "all
Governments and authorities" to issue a cease-fire order within
thirty-six hours. One week later, on May 29, it called upon
them again, this time "to order a cessation of all acts of armed
force for a period of four weeks." The Mediator, Count Folke
Bernadotte, was instructed "to make contact with all parties as
soon as the cease-fire is in force with a view to carrying out his
functions as determined by the General Assembly." As long as
the Arabs were making reasonable headway militarily, they
rejected every call for a cease-fire or truce. In the second week
of June their progress was halted, and the Mediator was able
to fix June 11 as the date on which the four-week truce was to
begin. The Arabs needed this respite to rest and rally their
forces. When the Mediator proposed that the truce be prolonged, they refused to agree. On July 7 the Security Council
addressed "an urgent appeal to the interested parties to accept
in principle the prolongation of the truce for such period as
may be decided upon in consultation with the Mediator." This
proved of no avail, and fighting was resumed two days later.

On July 15 the Security Council,

> taking into consideration that the Provisional Government
> of Israel has indicated its acceptance in principle of a pro-
> longation of the truce in Palestine; that the States members
> of the Arab League have rejected successive appeals of the
> United Nations Mediator, and of the Security Council in its
> resolution of 7 July 1948, for the prolongation of the truce
> in Palestine; and that there has consequently developed a
> renewal of hostilities in Palestine,

determined that the situation in Palestine constituted a threat to the peace within the meaning of Article 39 of the Charter, ordered the Governments and authorities concerned to desist from further military action ("at a time to be determined by the Mediator, but in any event not later than three days from the date of the adoption of this resolution"), and declared that failure to comply with its order would demonstrate the existence of a breach of the peace, "requiring immediate consideration by the Security Council with a view to such further action under Chapter VII of the Charter as may be decided upon by the Council." In other words, the Security Council was considering the imposition of sanctions against the side which refused to stop fighting. It was, however, less the threat of sanctions than the catastrophic development of the military situation which moved the Arab Governments to agree to a new cease-fire on July 21. The ten days of war which followed their refusals to renew the truce had cost them vital ground. The "second truce" which now began was to last, broken by sporadic fighting, until it was superseded by the armistice.

Ever since his arrival on the scene early in June, the Mediator had been active, flying from capital to capital, and conferring during the first truce with representatives of the parties at Rhodes. Count Bernadotte did not spare himself, but he showed from the first that disinclination to talk to the Arabs categorically in terms of peace which has characterized the United Nations' approach to the problem ever since. When Israel made a formal peace offer in August, he was startled and reluctant to convey it to the Arab side. Instead, he continued to think in terms of the partition resolution of November 29, 1947, unable to grasp, or unwilling to concede, that the position had been altered fundamentally by the Arabs' attempt to kill that resolution by force. He believed that Israel owed the Arabs something for the territory she held beyond the jigsaw puzzle of 1947, and perhaps for existing at all. He never took into account the fact that Israel held this territory only as a result of her successful defense against Arab attack, nor did he appear to believe that the Arabs owed Israel anything for the destruction and loss of life they had caused by their assault on her independence—and on the authority of the United Nations. As a result, he began to put forward "compromise" proposals of the kind that were to bedevil the issue for years. He suggested that in return for western Galilee Israel should give up the Negev, which had been allocated to her under the partition settlement. She was to surrender it to one of the aggressors, Jordan, as a land bridge to connect Egypt with the rest of the Arab world. Echoes of this proposal were to reverberate down the years; until the Sinai campaign of 1956, Egypt never tired of demanding the surrender of the southern Negev. Equally ill-advised, the Mediator at one stage suggested that Jerusalem be handed over to King Abdullah of Jordan. Proposals of this kind—maladroit at best, but widely regarded as sinister, reflecting British ambitions—inevitably roused the anger of the Israel public. On September 17 a group of fanatics assassinated Count Bernadotte in Jerusalem, by their action jeopardizing the stability of Israel more gravely than the Mediator could ever have done with his territorial proposals.

Renewed fighting in the autumn led to further debate in the Security Council. On November 4 the Council called upon the "interested Governments" to withdraw their forces to positions they had occupied three weeks before. Twelve days later, in a resolution which was to be the prelude to Rhodes, it decided on the establishment of an armistice.

The events of 1948 revealed in embryo all the difficulties that were to dog the United Nations, and all the incapacity it was to show, in its handling of Israel-Arab relations during the next ten years.

Having decided, after prolonged investigation and debate,

on the partition of Palestine and the establishment of independent Jewish and Arab states, the General Assembly took fright at the first sign of trouble. When it became apparent that the Arabs were prepared to use violence to defeat its objects, the Assembly, instead of insisting on loyal compliance, began to cast about for a new policy. The United States came up with the brainwave of trusteeship, which the Assembly would without a doubt have adopted if it had not, in effect, talked itself out. When zero hour struck on May 14, one organ of the Assembly was still trying to implement partition, the Assembly itself was preparing to accept trusteeship, the British mandate came to an end, Israel was established, and the Arab invasion began. If it had been left to the United Nations, Israel would not have come into existence that day. It was by the will of her people and the resolution of her leaders that she achieved her independence. When the Arab states, ostensibly to "restore law and order in Palestine," launched their invasion, she was left to deal with them as best she could, single-handed.

The Security Council was not at that time under the disability that was to stultify it later. The United States and the Soviet Union were both on the side of the angels. But it was not until July 15, after it had been provoked beyond endurance, that the Council was prepared to recognize, guardedly even then, that the Arab states were responsible for what was happening. It never got to the point of calling aggression aggression. In the end it could take some credit for stopping the fighting, but it is doubtful whether the Arabs would in fact have stopped if they had not seen that to continue would be militarily disastrous. The Security Council's call for an armistice met with no response from the Arab side until their military position had deteriorated even further, beyond repair.

Rhodes: the Armistice Agreements

On November 16, 1948, the Security Council of the United Nations, which for six months had confined itself to orders for cease-fire and truce, decided "that, in order to eliminate the threat to the peace in Palestine and to facilitate the transition from the present Truce to permanent peace in Palestine, an armistice shall be established in all sectors of Palestine." It called "upon the parties directly involved in the conflict in Palestine, as a further provisional measure under Article 40 of the Charter, to seek agreement forthwith, by negotiations conducted either directly or through the Acting Mediator on Palestine, with a view to the immediate establishment of the Armistice including:

(a) the delineation of permanent armistice demarcation lines beyond which the armed forces of the respective parties shall not move;

(b) such withdrawal and reduction of their armed forces as will ensure the maintenance of the armistice during the transition to permanent peace in Palestine."

There could be no question of direct negotiations. No Arab state has ever been willing to negotiate "directly" with Israel— that is, without benefit of United Nations intervention. But neither were the Arabs in any hurry to negotiate through the Acting Mediator, Dr. Ralph Bunche, the distinguished member of the United Nations Secretariat who had been Count Bernadotte's principal assistant. Only after another round of fighting had forced its army back into the Sinai desert did the Egyptian Government finally decide that an armistice might after all be acceptable. Syria still held parts of Israel territory and saw no need to parley, while weak Lebanon and Jordan could hardly take the initiative in negotiating as long as Egypt, the ringleader, held back. Israel had been ready for an armistice from the start, but she could do nothing as long as there was no one to negotiate with. So it was Egypt, on the Arab side, which broke the ice. The fighting in Sinai ended on January 7, 1949. Five days later negotiations began at Rhodes, conveniently neutral and isolated, yet within easy distance of Israel and Egypt alike.

We arrived at Rhodes in a United Nations Dakota which took off from the small airstrip just north of Tel Aviv; Lydda Airport, won back six months earlier with the defeat of the Arab Legion, was still not fully serviceable.

Dr. Bunche and his staff had set up their headquarters and living accommodations in one wing of the spacious Hotel des Roses and had reserved the other for the Egyptian and Israeli delegations. Israel occupied the larger part of one floor, and

Egypt the floor immediately above. It was an excellent arrangement. All the parties concerned in the negotiations were under the same roof, yet each enjoyed almost perfect privacy.

We saw at once that the Egyptian delegates were in no very friendly mood. When they saw an Israeli approaching in the corridor downstairs, they would eye him, literally, askance—demonstratively turning away their heads, though soon overcome by curiosity and turning back sufficiently to catch a glimpse. Dr. Bunche's early efforts to get us to meet were rebuffed by the Egyptians, until he made it clear that we had all come to negotiate, and that this meant meeting to talk things over. We met, the following day, in Dr. Bunche's sitting room, with the Acting Mediator himself presiding from his sofa, and the delegations of Israel and Egypt grouped on chairs to the right and left of him respectively. At first, the Egyptians insisted on addressing all their remarks to Dr. Bunche, as if we were not in the room, but it was impossible to keep up an artificiality of this kind, and the atmosphere soon improved. It was not long before the delegations were arguing with one another directly, in English and in French.

In the course of the six weeks we spent together at the Hotel des Roses, we became quite friendly with the Egyptians. Their earlier attitude may have been due to insecurity and shyness, or to instructions; I am certain it was not caused by any deep-seated hostility. We did not meet socially much, but when Abdul Moneim Mustafa, the chief political adviser on the Egyptian delegation,* fell ill, we sat at his bedside and comforted him; and when the armistice agreement was finally signed, Dr. Bunche had us all to a gay party in the evening, for which the Egyptians had sent a special plane from Cairo with

---

* He later became Minister of Egypt at Berne and an assistant secretary-general of the Arab League. Early in 1957 he turned up in a new part, as a member of King Saud's entourage on the state visit to Washington.

delicacies from Groppi's. I well remember sitting with the head of the Egyptian delegation, as he showed me photographs of his family, including one, with special pride, of his son who had just been commissioned as a second lieutenant in the Egyptian army. It was an atmosphere as different as one could imagine from that of the first day in the corridor, with its averted heads.

We felt that night, and I am fairly sure the Egyptians did too, that we had not only brought the fighting phase to a formal end, but had laid the foundations, if not of love and affection, at least of normal relations between our two countries. We all knew that the UN Conciliation Commission for Palestine (PCC), which had been set up by the General Assembly two and a half months earlier, was waiting, in the wings, as it were, to carry the armistice forward to peace. In fact, at various stages during the Rhodes neogtiations the PCC had shown signs of impatience, prodding Dr. Bunche to ask how we were getting on and when *they* might expect to take over. Dr. Bunche had reacted with some asperity, making it clear that one thing had to be done at a time and that he resented their interference.

Dr. Bunche, indeed, took a realistic view of the situation throughout. He probably had fewer illusions than any of us. He not only preached the doctrine of "one thing at a time," but he practiced it. While we were negotiating with the Egyptians, the Governments of Jordan and Lebanon intimated that they too would like to join in the negotiations. Dr. Bunche replied that they would have to wait until the agreement between Israel and Egypt was concluded. He understood that separate negotiations between Israel and each of the Arab states were a condition for success. The PCC unfortunately did not grasp this when they took over from him after the agreements with Egypt, Lebanon and Jordan were signed and so, as will be seen, with their own hands sowed the seeds of their failure.

31

Dr. Bunche, as a mediator in the circumstances prevailing at that time, was ideal. He was gifted, some thought almost a genius, at drafting; sooner or later he was able to contrive a formula to defeat almost any problem. It was not his fault if the experience of the following years showed that formulas were not enough to preserve the peace, or even an armistice, if the will to preserve it was lacking. If the delegations set the pace, Dr. Bunche set the tone. The armistice agreement with Egypt was negotiated on the assumption that its place would soon be taken by a treaty of peace. Article I of the agreement states, in part:

> With a view to promoting the return of permanent peace in Palestine and in recognition of the importance in this regard of mutual assurances concerning the future military operations of the parties, the following principles . . . are hereby affirmed:
> . . . 4. The establishment of an armistice between the armed forces of the two Parties is accepted as an indispensable step toward the liquidation of armed conflict and the restoration of peace in Palestine.

Dr. Bunche never lost sight of the immediate goal, which, limited as it was (to an armistice), long seemed remote and perhaps unattainable. At the same time, he understood that the armistice was an essential step in the transition from truce to peace. He knew when to be persuasive and gentle, when to be firm, and even when it paid to be sardonic or gruff. He had had the pleasant notion of ordering from a local manufacturer two sets of the decorated ceramic plates for which Rhodes is famous. Each member of the two delegations and of his own staff was to receive such a plate, inscribed "Rhodes Armistice Talks 1949," as a memento when the agreement was signed. At one point we floundered in what seemed insuperable difficulties.

Dr. Bunche called us into his room, opened a chest of drawers and showed us the plates, about which until then we had known nothing; they had been intended as a surprise. "Have a look at these lovely plates!" he said. "If you reach agreement, each of you will get one to take home. If you don't, I'll break them over your heads!" When we signed the armistice, Dr. Bunche's prize-giving duly took place. These plates still adorn many an office or home in Jerusalem, and perhaps, despite later events, in Cairo too.

The Egyptian-Israeli General Armistice Agreement, signed on February 24, 1949, is (like the later agreements with Lebanon, Jordan and Syria) as much a political as a military instrument. This dual nature—of the negotiations and of the agreement to which they led—was accepted from the start by both sides. Their understanding of the enterprise on which they were engaged was reflected in the composition of the delegations, each of which consisted of political and military officers. But perhaps it was not altogether a matter of chance that while the head of Israel's delegation was the Director-General of her Foreign Ministry, assisted by senior military and legal advisers, the Egyptian delegation was led by a brigadier, supported by a military staff (which included the brother-in-law of King Farouk) as well as by political and legal consultants. At the time we did not read too much into this difference of emphasis, though naturally it did not escape us; and I do not think that too much need be read into it even now. In any case, each delegation operated as a well-knit unit, ready to tussle with the other and strike the best bargain it could.

Much of the armistice agreement was necessarily concerned with immediate military matters, such as the withdrawal and reduction of forces and the exchange of prisoners. But other aspects of the agreement were more fundamental; some were intended to be fundamental, and others have become so with the passing of time and the continued absence of a peace treaty.

The agreement defined the "armistice demarcation line," which, although "not to be construed in any sense as a political or territorial boundary," in fact became, and has been ever since, the frontier between Israel and Egypt. It was in this way that the Gaza "strip" came into existence; occupied at the time by Egyptian forces, it was recognized implicitly as Egyptian-held territory pending a final settlement. In general, the armistice demarcation line was drawn on the basis of the existing military situation, between the opposing armies. This principle, explicitly stated, later held good also for the agreements with Lebanon, Jordan and Syria, though in each of these cases there were deviations from it in practice.

The armistice agreement with Egypt created a demilitarized zone round the village of El Auja (Nitzana) in the Negev, in Israel territory. This zone, like the more complicated demilitarized areas established by the armistice agreement with Syria, subsequently became, and remains to this day, a source of conflict between Israel and her Arab neighbors. Its importance arises from its position at the junction of four roads, one linking it with the rest of Israel and three leading straight into Egypt. Egypt has come more and more to claim that this is a *neutral* zone which does not belong to Israel any more than it does to Egypt herself. Israel maintains that demilitarization does not affect sovereignty and that the El Auja zone is as much part of Israel as is the rest of the Negev, or the plain of Sharon, for that matter. When Egyptian army units occupied part of the demilitarized zone in October 1955 and refused to withdraw, Israel forces expelled them and have remained in El Auja ever since. After the Sinai campaign of November 1956 the Secretary-General of the United Nations proposed that the demilitarized zone be occupied by the UN Emergency Force (UNEF). The proposal was unacceptable to Israel, UNEF having no mandate on the Israel side of the border.

The demilitarization of the El Auja zone came about in a curious way. The Egyptian Government had kept its people in the dark about the army's defeat; it was commonly believed in Cairo, as late as January 1949, that Egyptian forces were within striking distance of Tel Aviv. Accordingly, when armistice negotiations began, the Egyptian delegates were under pressure to save face as best they could. They demanded that we agree to the appointment of an Egyptian military governor at Beersheba, in Israel. Egyptian troops had occupied this undefended town during the first days of the invasion in May 1948, but had been driven out of it in October and were by this time safely back on their own soil. The members of the Egyptian delegation were very insistent on this military governor, explaining that, stationed in a town in Israel, he would of course exercise no real powers, but that his appointment was essential for them as a matter of prestige and that without it they could not sign an armistice.

After a great deal of argument we persuaded them that their demand was absurd, whereupon they fell back on a new suggestion—that an Egyptian military governor be appointed at Bir Asluj. Bir Asluj was not much more than a group of mud huts, situated on the road from Beersheba to El Auja and Egypt. A military governor to preside over these mud huts was a fantastic idea, but the title "Military Governor of Bir Asluj" might have impressed readers of the Cairo press and so would have helped save the face of the Egyptian Government, which needed a military governor somewhere in Israel at any price— even, seemingly, at the price of making itself a laughingstock in the eyes of anyone outside, or inside, Egypt who knew exactly what Bir Asluj was.

We talked them out of this, mainly by ridicule. They came up next with the suggestion of an Egyptian military governor at El Auja, closer to the border but still in Israel. We rejected this demand as well, as we were bound to. We could not conceivably agree to Egypt's appointing a military governor anywhere on our territory, just as the Egyptians could never have agreed, had we suggested such a thing, to our appointing an Israeli military governor on theirs. Dr. Bunche saw that we could not accept their proposal, but he also felt that their need to save face was genuine. He accordingly suggested that Israel agree not to keep troops in El Auja, and that this, with a parallel commitment from Egypt, be written into the armistice agreement. The idea did not appeal at all to the Israel Government, but when it became clear that the successful conclusion of the armistice depended on it, the point was conceded.

In this way the demilitarized zone of El Auja came into existence, as the last faint relic of what was to have been an Egyptian military governor in Beersheba. It is possible, of course, that the Egyptian delegation never really expected us to agree to their appointment of a military governor at Beersheba, Bir Asluj or El Auja, but put up these demands as a roundabout way of bargaining for the demilitarization of this strategic zone. If this is so, they were certainly cunning and played their hand well.

Had it been thought at the time that the armistice agreement might not soon be supplanted by a more permanent treaty, its ban on the unauthorized crossing of the demarcation line would have been phrased less loosely. The agreement merely provided that "rules and regulations of the armed forces of the Parties, which prohibit civilians from crossing the fighting lines or entering the area between the lines, shall remain in effect after the signing of this Agreement with application to the Armistice Demarcation Line." The purpose of this clause was to avoid the disturbance that would be caused if civilians began moving unchecked in an area in which armies were still deployed, particularly in view of the many unsettled refugees for whom no provision had yet been made. That the troops of each country should remain where they were and not cross into the territory of the other was a matter of course: "the basic purpose of the Armistice Demarcation Line is to delineate the line beyond which the armed forces of the respective parties shall not move."

No one could have foreseen at the time that Egypt would in a few years turn Gaza into a base for systematic *fedayeen* action against Israel. Behind the shelter of the armistice demarcation line, Egypt built up a force of armed raiders, whose incursions into Israel territory became increasingly bold and destructive and led ultimately to counteraction by Israel. "Reprisal raids" pacified the area for a time, but as Egyptian attacks across the demarcation line assumed severer form and cost many lives, Israel inevitably planned to demolish the *fedayeen* base itself. Villagers in the border zones could not be protected against the deliberate *fedayeen* policy of the Nasser Government by an armistice agreement which had been drafted nearly eight years before. On November 3, 1956, Israel forces captured Gaza. Many of the *fedayeen* were caught, others died in the fighting or were driven back into Egypt. Their base was destroyed.

The armistice agreement with Egypt contains a clause, which became part of the agreements with Lebanon, Jordan and Syria as well, laying down procedure for its revision, if this should become necessary:

> The Parties to this Agreement may, by mutual consent, revise this Agreement or any of its provisions, or may suspend its application, other than Articles I and II,* at any time. In the absence of mutual agreement and after this Agreement

---

* Articles I and II were those which established the fact of the armistice and laid down its principles. The remaining articles contained detailed provisions for its implementation. The first two articles were essentially political, the rest mostly military.

has been in effect for one year from the date of its signing, either of the Parties may call upon the Secretary-General of the United Nations to convene a conference of representatives of the two Parties for the purpose of reviewing, revising or suspending any of the provisions of this Agreement other than Articles I and II. Participation in such conference shall be obligatory on the Parties.

There was never, subsequently, any question of "mutual consent." It became the firm policy of Egypt and the other Arab states not to negotiate with Israel, directly or indirectly, on revision of the armistice or anything else. Israel once invoked this clause, in the case of Jordan, in November 1953. Though participation in a conference with Israel was obligatory, Jordan refused the Secretary-General's repeated invitations. Israel, in accordance with the procedure laid down in the armistice agreement, referred the matter to the Security Council. The Council devoted several meetings to a complicated procedural discussion, which led to no result. The United Nations was powerless in the face of Jordan's recalcitrance. It was clear that this clause of the armistice agreement was fated to remain a dead letter, and Israel never again invoked it. Renewed attempts to bring about the revision of an agreement which had long outlived its original relevance and purpose could only have led to further useless wrangling in the Security Council. Jordan, by refusing the Secretary-General's invitation, had committed a clear breach of the agreement, and Israel had to be content to leave it at that, defining it as "an international transgression of unusual scope and gravity."

The "revision clause" conferred on each party the right, if there was no mutual consent, to call upon the Secretary-General to convene a conference with the other *after the agreement had been in effect for one year*. This did not mean that its authors assumed from the start that the agreement would

remain in force for as much as a year. It meant that they realized that if by some unforeseen chance, and contrary to all expectation, the agreement was not replaced by a peace treaty
within the year, it would stand in urgent need of revision. It
was accepted that the agreement, as it stood, would become out-
dated after twelve months, and that provision had to be made
for "reviewing, revising or suspending" any part of it that did
not stand the test of time. No one knew exactly when permanent peace would take the place of the armistice. It might
be ten weeks, or conceivably ten months. That the armistice
would have to make do for ten years would have occurred to
no one.

Not many days after the armistice agreement with Egypt was
signed, a second round of negotiations began at Rhodes—with
Jordan. A new delegation of Israel took the place of the one
that had negotiated the first agreement, differing from it in
composition but not in quality. The quality of the Jordanian
delegates, however, was not equal to the mission on which they
had been dispatched. The Egyptian delegation had been skill-
ful, tenacious and well briefed. That of Lebanon was fully
adequate to its task, which proved the easiest of all. The delegates of Syria were fiercely argumentative, evidently regarding
diplomacy as a form of aggression, and were well able to stand
up for the rights of their country.

Jordan's delegation, however, was not of this mettle. When
they arrived at Rhodes, they were seen to be an unimpressive
set. They looked helpless and lost, apparently not sure of their
instructions; it seemed possible, indeed, that no clear instructions had been given them. King Abdullah, their master, soon
indicated that he did not trust them to negotiate on his behalf
and that he proposed to take matters in hand himself. It was
agreed that the talks at Rhodes should continue as a façade,
but that the real negotiations should be conducted in secret

with the King at his winter palace at Shuneh. Only the King's closest confidants were to know; the rest of the world was to go on watching the show at Rhodes. This had, perhaps, been the King's intention from the outset and determined his choice of delegates.

The conversations at Shuneh will not quickly be forgotten by those who took part in them. There was the excitement of traveling in enemy territory under cover of night. We crossed each time on foot through the barricades of no man's land in Jerusalem, to find a car and an escort waiting for us on the other side. The proceedings at Shuneh consisted invariably of a general talk before dinner and more detailed discussion afterward, until early in the morning. The time limit for each night's talk was set by the necessity of returning across the frontier before dawn.

The meetings with King Abdullah were held in a long room embellished with an oil painting of the battle of Trafalgar, the gift of King George V. The King sat at one end on a dais, with his ministers to his right and some of his advisers on low stools facing him. The Israelis were on his left. A British officer of the Arab Legion, Glubb Pasha's chief of operations, was present from beginning to end. King Abdullah, not a tall man, was in every other respect head and shoulders above his entourage. He was eloquent, gentle yet forceful, self-confident, optimistic, even something of an idealist; he wore the quick, easy smile of a charmer. By contrast, his ministers and advisers made little impression, though they must have been habile politicians, since most of them have continued to hold high office, despite all the crises and changes which have overtaken their country. It would not be fair to name them, lest they share the fate which overtook their King, but Abdullah Tell is an exception. This man, long King Abdullah's favorite, was later condemned to death for his part in the King's assassination; fortunately for him, he had by that time fled the country and could read his sentence in the Cairo papers. Tell, accustomed to delicate missions, was detailed by the King to meet us in no man's land and escort us to Shuneh. At the Shuneh talks he stood out from the rest of the King's advisers, maintaining an attitude of utter cynicism, yet helping actively to secure agreement with Israel. He seemed to be wholly without illusions about the Arabs, the British and everyone else. He spoke about the King, even in the King's presence, in a way which could be described only as contemptuous, and yet he seemed to feel affection for him and to be genuinely anxious to safeguard his interests.

The results achieved at Shuneh were transmitted by each party to its delegation at Rhodes and were incorporated in the armistice agreement signed there on April 3, 1949. The demarcation line was not drawn strictly in accordance with the position of the armies, but further east. It involved the cession to Israel of considerable territory, the governing factors being in the main topographical. The Jordanians were anxious to keep as many villages as possible on their side of the line, but they cared less about village lands. As a result, a good many farmers were cut off from their land, and some from their wells. Here again, however, this was regarded as a temporary expedient, pending peace and the establishment of a definitive frontier. It is not likely that either Israel or Jordan would have agreed to this particular demarcation line except as a provisional measure. As such, it would not have inflicted on local farmers more than the minimum hardship that follows inevitably from war, and it would not have served in later years as a constant magnet to "infiltrators" and a source of periodic conflict between the two countries.

The armistice agreement with Jordan followed the same general pattern as that with Egypt, but it left one group of problems unresolved. These were to be considered, after the signing of the agreement, by a joint special committee set up under Article VIII to formulate "agreed plans and arrangements designed to enlarge the scope of this Agreement and to effect improvements in its application." The special committee, which was established because the necessary "plans and arrangements" had not been worked out fully in the course of the negotiations, was to deal immediately with certain specified problems, including "resumption of the normal functioning of the cultural and humanitarian institutions on Mount Scopus and free access thereto" and "free access to the Holy Places and cultural institutions and use of the cemetery on the Mount of Olives." Despite all pressure by Israel, it has never been possible to get this special committee to work. Jordan's refusal to meet and formulate the "agreed plans and arrangements" envisaged by Article VIII represents a standing breach of the armistice agreement. The unsolved problems are a constant menace to security, particularly the problem of access to Mount Scopus, an Israeli enclave in Jordanian territory, manned by a small force of police who are relieved once a fortnight under arrangements made by the United Nations. The "cultural and humanitarian institutions" on Mount Scopus include Jerusalem's largest hospital and the Hebrew University, both of which have been inaccessible since 1948. The National and University Library, with over a million books, has not had a reader for ten years. Jordan has not even allowed the transfer of books to the library's new premises in Jerusalem. The question of implementing Article VIII has been taken up repeatedly with the United Nations, so far without success. No organ of the United Nations has ever been keen to tackle an Arab state on compliance with the armistice.

King Abdullah, alone of the Arab rulers, was sincere in regarding the armistice as a step toward peace. After the agreement was signed, he sought a more permanent arrangement with Israel. Conversations with him and some of his closest advisers were carried on intensively, specially between November 1949 and March 1950. A draft treaty was prepared and initiated, but the King, under the rising pressure of an Arab extremism which scared his ministers, was unable in the end to carry it through. Desultory talks went on, but after a while it became clear that nothing could come of them, despite the personal efforts of the King and the concessions which Israel was ready to make. Talks carried on, sometimes daily, over so long a period could not remain an absolute secret, and in the course of time it came to be suspected that the King was planning to make peace with Israel. This, in the eyes of Arab "nationalists," was treason. King Abdullah was murdered on the threshold of the Mosque of Omar on July 20, 1951. His death served as a warning to others, and nowhere in the Arab camp has there been talk of peace with Israel since.

Negotiations for the armistice with Lebanon were conducted without incident at Rosh Hanikra, a rocky headland on the frontier. The agreement was signed on March 23, 1949. Its most noteworthy feature arose from the fact that Israeli forces, in repelling Lebanese attacks, had carried the war into Lebanon and occupied fourteen villages. Under the terms of the agreement, the armistice demarcation line was established on the old international frontier and was made identical with it. This meant the withdrawal of Israel's troops from the Lebanese territory they had occupied. Israel undertook to do this—and in fact did so, unconditionally—but she expected that Syria, which had occupied parts of Israeli territory in the same general area, would do likewise. In this she was to be disappointed, Syria not considering herself bound by the Lebanese precedent. The Arab states invaded Israel together, but each made its armistice separately. For the armistice agreement with Lebanon it can at least be said that it has not been seriously undermined by later events. Lebanon has never again shown any inclination to attack Israel and has, by and large, been meticulous in observance of the agreement. The agreement with Lebanon shows, indeed, what the armistice with each of the other Arab states might have been, even in the absence of peace, had these states not turned them to political and military account for the prosecution of the war against Israel by other means.

The case of Syria was very different. Syria was reluctant to negotiate at all, partly because of an inherent fanaticism, partly because she feared that any agreement must provide for the withdrawal of her forces from the areas in Israel which they had invaded and still held. The agreements with Egypt, Lebanon and Jordan had been signed within a period of less than six weeks, and all were concluded by the first days of April. Negotiations with Syria did not begin till April 5 and dragged on, at times it seemed interminably, until July 20, when the agreement was at last signed. The meetings between the two delegations were held under stifling conditions, in the heat of summer, in a tent pitched athwart the Tiberias–Damascus highway, near Mishmar Hayarden, in the no man's land between the opposing camps.

After wearisome argument the Syrians were persuaded to withdraw their forces from Israel territory, but they stipulated that Israeli forces should not replace theirs in the evacuated areas. In this way another demilitarized zone was created. This might have been tolerable if the armistice were but a provisional instrument, as was intended at the time. A peace treaty would have established definitive frontiers; the armistice agreement stipulated expressly that "the . . . arrangements for the Armistice Demarcation Line . . . are not to be interpreted as having any relation whatsoever to ultimate territorial arrangements affecting the two Parties."

As it was, an extremely complicated situation was created. It so happened that some of Israel's main development projects were to be carried out, and had indeed been begun, in the vicinity of the Syrian border. The drainage of Lake Huleh and the realignment of the Jordan bed called for extensive digging, bridging and other engineering work, some of it in the newly demilitarized zone. As in the case of El Auja, Israel maintained that demilitarization did not detract from her sovereignty and relied on the clause in the agreement which recognized "the gradual restoration of normal civilian life in the area of the Demilitarized Zone" as a basic aim of the armistice. Syria, though unable to claim the demilitarized zone for herself, denied Israel's sovereignty over it, regarding it apparently as a kind of no man's land in which Israel was not entitled to do anything without Syrian consent. She also held that Israel's development projects prejudiced the "ultimate settlement" and conferred on Israel a military advantage, contrary to the terms of the agreement.

Ever since 1951,* this demilitarized zone has been a source

---

* "Early in 1951 another complaint was brought before the Security Council, this time by Syria. Relating to drainage schemes intended to reclaim the Huleh marshes and to conserve precious water supplies, this complaint was formally based on the provisions of the Israel-Syrian Armistice Agreement establishing a demilitarized zone in a small area bordering the Jordan River. This small portion of Israel territory had been occupied by Syrian forces during the fighting in 1948. The demilitarized zone was formed in 1949 when, under the Armistice Agreement, they agreed to return to their side of the frontier on condition that the Israel armed forces would not reoccupy the area evacuated. Israel accepted this solution—which had been proposed by the Acting Mediator—on the understanding that normal civilian life in the demilitarized zone would not be prejudiced thereby, and that the development of the country's meagre natural resources, particularly water supplies, would not be interfered with. The Syrian complaint to the Council was in fact an attempt to stifle Israel's development plans. . . . The situation was complicated by difficulties of interpretation, one of the points of disagreement being the *locus standi* of Syria in a matter concerning a demilitarized zone entirely situated on Israel territory in which, in accordance with the Armistice Agreement, normal

of conflict. No other Arab claim arising under the armistice agreements has been pursued with such tenacity and venom. It has been argued repeatedly before the Security Council, usually with unsatisfactory results or no results at all. The pattern has generally been the same. Israel proceeds with a development project. Syria protests and seeks to stop it. Israel does not admit Syria's right to veto or interfere with any peaceful activity on which she is engaged within her own borders. Syria thereupon uses force, if she has not done so in the first place, her military outposts along the demarcation line firing at workers and engineers on the Israeli side. The United Nations steps in and, with an appearance of objectivity, stops both the shooting and the development work.

This explanation perhaps simplifies a complex problem, but it is essentially true. In fact, all work on the Jordan water scheme in the demilitarized zone has been held up since 1953. In a characteristic resolution adopted on October 27 of that year, the Security Council,

> *desirous* of facilitating the consideration of the question, without however prejudicing the rights, claims or positions of the parties concerned,
>
> *deems* it desirable to that end that the works started in the Demilitarized Zone on 2 September 1953 should be suspended during the urgent examination of the question by the Security Council,
>
> *notes* with satisfaction the statement made by the Israel repre-

---

civilian activities were being conducted. More important, however, was the underlying dispute and the Syrian attempt to harness the authority of the Security Council in support of the proposition that United Nations machinery should be available to prevent normal development for the improvement of living standards." *Israel and the United Nations* (New York, Carnegie Endowment for International Peace, 1956), pp. 105–6.

sentative . . . regarding the undertaking given by his Government to suspend the works in question during that examination,

requests the Chief of Staff of the Truce Supervision Organization to inform it regarding the fulfillment of that undertaking.

This resolution represented a complete victory for Syria, reasonably as it was worded on the face of it. The Israel Government, to create the opportunity for a peaceful solution without shooting or the threat of shooting from the Syrian side, had offered to suspend work temporarily and so make it possible to discuss the issue calmly. Its offer was accepted by the Security Council, which was to study the question as a matter of urgency. But the Council's "urgent examination" has still not been undertaken and certainly not been completed, with the result that vital development works have been held up for over four years. Any suggestion by Israel that she has allowed more than ample time for "urgent examination of the question" by the Security Council, and that she now feels herself free to resume work, is met by immediate threats from Syria. To preserve the peace, Israel has had to concentrate for the time being on work elsewhere. But the issue remains unresolved and may any day lead to open conflict. As long as Syria sees that she can exploit the irresolution of the Security Council in her constant endeavor to hamper the development of Israel, no one will expect her to allow such opportunities to slip.

The conclusion of the armistice agreements was received with relief by the entire world and hailed as a triumph for the United Nations. At the same time more modest tribute was paid to the good sense of the parties concerned. Dr. Bunche was awarded the Nobel Peace Prize for his part in bringing the agreements about, and it was universally conceded that the

47

honor was deserved. The Security Council passed a congratulatory resolution praising him, Count Bernadotte and their staff. Yet it was mainly the impact of a given military situation that produced the agreements. Israel's success in repelling the invader left the Arab states with no choice but to accept an armistice and secure the best terms they could. They bargained shrewdly and achieved more than they can have expected. It is certain that they would not have achieved as much if Israel had not had a political interest in conciliating them as far as she could, and if the Conciliation Commission had not begun working toward the next stage——peace.

The armistice agreements could not survive, except nominally, against the mounting tide of Arab nationalism and extremism. Like all agreements, they had real validity only as long as the parties concerned found them useful, and only to the extent that they did not interfere with overriding national policies. They could probably not have been concluded at all if the "cold war" had in 1949 attained the proportions it has attained since, specifically in the Middle East. If the United States had been backing one side, and the Soviet Union the other, no agreement could ever have come about. It was a fortunate chance that at that particular time none of the Great Powers had an active interest in fomenting trouble between Israel and the Arab states. All seemed concerned to see the fighting brought to an end and foundations laid for a permanent peace.

3

Lausanne: the Conciliation Effort

DURING THE GREATER PART of 1948 the Security Council and the General Assembly took turns in considering the "Palestine Question." For much of the time they were, indeed, discussing it simultaneously, without getting too much in one another's way. The Security Council naturally concerned itself mainly with the military aspects of the situation and attempted, on two notable occasions with success, to put an end to the actual fighting. The General Assembly debated the possibilities of a political settlement, finding itself at times, amid the rapid succession of events, singularly out of touch with realities.

On December 11, 1948, the General Assembly, "having considered further the situation in Palestine," adopted an omnibus resolution, whose main feature was the establishment of a Conciliation Commission (the PCC). This Commission was to consist of "three States Members of the United Nations," to be chosen on the recommendation of the permanent members of the Security Council, acting *ad hoc* as a committee of the Assembly. The three states chosen were France, the United States and Turkey. They constitute the PCC to this day.

Under the terms of the General Assembly's resolution, the PCC was to assume, "as far as it considers necessary in existing circumstances," the functions of the United Nations Mediator. This explains the Commission's constant prodding of Dr. Bunche at Rhodes and his riposte of *festina lente*. It was, of course, to the Commission's credit, as well as in accordance with the Assembly's instructions, that it was anxious to begin its work as soon as possible. The task it had been set was complex. It was to carry out "the specific functions and directives given to it by the present resolution and such additional functions and directives as may be given to it by the General Assembly or by the Security Council."

The specific functions included "the establishment of contact between the parties themselves and the Commission at the earliest possible date." The Commission was instructed "to take steps to assist the Governments and authorities concerned to achieve a final settlement of all questions outstanding between them," while these "Governments and authorities" were called upon, for their part, "to extend the scope of the negotiations provided for in the Security Council's resolution of 16 November 1948 and to seek agreement by negotiations conducted either with the Conciliation Commission or directly with a view to the final settlement of all questions outstanding between them."

The General Assembly did not call explicitly for peace between Israel and the Arab states. In this respect, as in others, the Security Council had been bolder: it had not hesitated to set "permanent peace" as the goal. When the General Assembly looked to "the final settlement of all questions outstanding" between the parties and called upon them "to extend the scope" of armistice negotiations which had not yet begun, it meant the same thing; but it chose, from deference to Arab feeling, a periphrastic way of expressing itself. Ever since, the term "peace" has been all but taboo in the United Nations' dealings with the Arab states, for fear of causing offense; and for the same reason the Great Powers have, in this context, mostly been careful too to avoid use of so embarrassing a word.

The Commission was instructed further to deal with two elaborately defined questions, those of Jerusalem and the refugees, and was given general directives on how to approach them. It was to prepare detailed proposals for a permanent international regime for the Jerusalem area and to concern itself with the Holy Places in general. As regards the refugees, it was instructed to facilitate their "repatriation, resettlement and economic and social rehabilitation" and the payment of compensation. In addition, the Commission was "to seek arrangements . . . which will facilitate the economic development of the area, including arrangements for access to ports and airfields and the use of transportation and communication facilities." It was, lastly, authorized "to appoint such subsidiary bodies and to employ such technical experts, acting under its authority, as it may find necessary for the effective discharge of its functions and responsibilities." It was to have its official headquarters at Jerusalem. In the course of time it met there, at Beirut, at Lausanne, at Geneva, at Paris and at New York.

The Commission had been given a difficult task to discharge, but it made it more difficult, and probably doomed it to failure from the outset, by its own early mistakes. It set up its headquarters at Jerusalem on January 24, 1949, moving soon afterward to Beirut for consultation with the representatives of the Arab states. Here was its first fatal error. It welded the Arabs into a single group for purposes of negotiation with Israel and with itself. Later, the Commission reported to the General Assembly that it had not contemplated "assembling the representatives of the two (sic!) parties around one table or even under the same roof." It saw no contradiction between this and the Assembly's call for "the establishment of contact between the parties themselves," deciding that "contact" meant merely "facilitating the exchange of views."

The Arabs needed no further encouragement not to negotiate directly with Israel. Taking their cue from the PCC, they remained obstinate in their refusal to meet representatives of Israel face to face, though they had of course done so in the armistice negotiations. Dr. Bunche had been insistent on negotiating each agreement directly between Israel and the Arab state concerned. "Two parties," for him, meant Israel and Egypt, Israel and Lebanon, Israel and Jordan, Israel and Syria. It did not mean Israel on the one hand and, on the other, all the Arab states combined. The Arabs had accepted this arrangement without demur and had, indeed, proposed no other. It was only when the PCC gave them their chance that they insisted on appearing as a single "party" and, as such, refused to meet the other.

The appearance of the Arabs as a single party inevitably made them, individually and thus collectively, more intransigent. The representatives of Egypt, Jordan, Lebanon and Syria never met the PCC except in a body. The Commission not only tolerated this arrangement but encouraged it. The result was, naturally, that any Arab representative who may have had relatively moderate views on a given subject was intimidated. He would not dare to express in the presence of three colleagues from the other Arab countries any opinion that these might consider weak or treasonable, even if his opinion was sincerely held and might well have been discussed if he were meeting representatives of Israel, or even the Conciliation Commission, alone. In this way the Commission pushed the Arabs along the path of extremism, from which, spurred also by other forces, they have never since looked back.

The PCC soon invited the parties to a conference at Lausanne, Switzerland. The conference opened on April 27, 1949, after all the armistice agreements except that with Syria had been signed. It dragged on, increasingly lifeless, until September. Under the conditions created by the Commission itself there was never a chance that anything could be done. At Rhodes, Egypt and Israel, later Jordan and Israel, had been housed under the same roof. Together with Dr. Bunche and his staff, we all lived, ate, worked and played billiards in the Hotel des Roses. At Lausanne, the Arab delegations were accommodated together at the Lausanne Palace in the upper part of the town, while Israel and the Commission were far away at the Beau Rivage on the lakeside at Ouchy. There was no opportunity for informal contact—until it was created, in secret, by the Arabs themselves.

When the Arab delegations appeared in a body at Lausanne, declaring that they would refuse to sit at the same table or in the same room as Israel, the Commission should have told them at once that in such circumstances there could be no conference and that everyone had better go home. Perhaps the delegation of Israel, too, should have said that in view of the Arabs' attitude it saw no point in remaining. The General Assembly's resolution did, indeed, envisage negotiations "conducted either with the Conciliation Commission or directly," but if the Arabs were to negotiate with the Commission alone, there was no point in calling the other party all the way from Jerusalem to Lausanne, or indeed in meeting at Lausanne at all. Such negotiations could have been carried on at Beirut, where they had begun. It must have been the Commission's intention, in convening a conference on neutral ground, that the parties should meet—that is, that there should really be a *conference*. Actually, Lausanne was never a conference at all, certainly not a conference between Israel and the Arab states; at the most, the PCC "conferred" with each party separately. Throughout the five months, representatives of Israel and the Arab states never met officially even once.

The Lausanne "conference" was a tragic farce. I can recall no experience more frustrating. It was made worse by the contrast between the inspiring beauty of the Lake of Geneva, an ideal setting for creative thought, and the hollow sham of the proceedings at the green baize table of the PCC. Almost the only relief was afforded by the efforts of each Arab delegation to make secret contact with that of Israel. Each was determined to meet the Israelis, but only on condition that the others should not know about it. They took elaborate precautions. On several occasions I met the head of one Arab delegation in a small restaurant near the funicular station at Ouchy, but never before ten o'clock at night. He would not leave the Lausanne Palace until it was dark, for fear the others might see him go. The head of another Arab delegation, an old friend from Rhodes, would meet us in the late afternoon at a café in Pully village, well outside Lausanne, where he felt sure no one would spot him. Members of the two remaining delegations were more timid, or perhaps more enterprising: they insisted that their meetings with us take place in Paris. In this way we held regular unofficial meetings with all the Arab representatives, each of whom was sure the others knew nothing about them. They were all anxious, in particular, that members of the Commission should not learn of these trysts, which made nonsense of their refusal to meet us under official auspices. Nothing came of our meetings—they could not be reconciled with the declared policies and actions of the Arab states. But we grew to know some of our Arab colleagues well, and they spoke with us frankly.

After the experience of Beirut and this early taste of the

Arabs' mood, the Conciliation Commission was in something of a quandary how best to open the proceedings at Lausanne. In meeting first with one side and then with the other, it realized it would have to have something to meet about, and if possible to give. The Commission had nothing whatever in its own gift and had therefore to look around for contributions. Its chairman at that time was Mr. Mark Ethridge, the American member; the chairmanship went by monthly rotation. On the evening of our arrival he invited me to his room for a private talk. He said the Arabs were being unhelpful (the term he used was stronger) and the atmosphere was bad. To improve it and set the ball rolling, Israel should make a concession, without asking for anything in return. For example, it would make a great impression on the Arabs and send the conference off to a good start if Israel were willing to do something to ease the worst hardships of the refugees. As a result of the fighting, many refugee families were split. Parents had sent their children to safety and now found them cut off on the other side of the lines; similarly, in the confusion of war, husbands had become separated from their wives. Mr. Ethridge believed it would be a great humanitarian act, and would profoundly move the Arab delegates, if Israel agreed to the return of such refugees. The Arabs could hardly fail to respond to such a gesture. After consulting our Government, we agreed. Mr. Ethridge and his colleagues were delighted and grateful. The Arabs were not. They were disdainful and indifferent. This was the origin of the "reunion of families" scheme, under which the Israel Government has admitted some six thousand refugees. To this day there is a trickle of Arabs who resume residence in Israel under this scheme—children, for instance, who on completing their schooling in some Arab country return to their parents' home.

The Arab delegations continued to harden their hearts. They were not impressed by Israel's gesture, seeing it only as a sign of weakness. The pattern was to be repeated throughout the drear months of Lausanne. The PCC felt, on second thought, that the reunion of families was perhaps not enough, even for a start, and accordingly made further suggestions. Israel agreed to pay compensation for Arab lands which had been abandoned and previously cultivated. She agreed to consider unfreezing the assets of Arab refugees held in Israeli banks. Under this scheme, a total of $10,000,000 was ultimately made available for payment and transfer to recipients in various Arab countries, in addition to the securities and valuables released from safe deposits. No genuine claim was refused. Finally, Israel agreed to the return of up to one hundred thousand refugees as a contribution toward the threefold aim of "repatriation, resettlement and economic and social rehabilitation."

All these gestures remained without response from the Arab side. The Arabs saw that, under the PCC's pressure, they could apparently rely on Israel's making concession after concession without their having to give anything in return. The only effect of these one-sided concessions by Israel was to convince the Arabs of the rightness of their policy and tactics. As time went on, Israel became more and more reluctant to make such concessions, and even the Commission came to see that they only stiffened the Arab attitude and made the prospects of any real success increasingly dim. As the Commission had no further ideas and had not managed to wring agreement out of the Arabs on even minor points, it decided to adjourn the conference. It had been an ill-starred venture from the first.

The Arabs insisted throughout that no general peace negotiations could be undertaken until the refugee question was settled. Israel was willing to discuss the refugee question but felt it could be solved only within the framework of a general settlement (the General Assembly's "final settlement of all questions outstanding between them"). This was the basic impasse of the conference. Some progress might have been made if the Arabs had been genuinely anxious to see the refugee problem solved, but it became clear at Lausanne that they had begun to grasp the worth of the refugees as a political asset and were not willing to see their numbers reduced. Hence their refusal of Israel's offer to repatriate the hundred thousand.

A few days after the conference opened, the representatives of three separate refugee groups appeared at Lausanne and asked for a hearing. These men were themselves refugees and had been elected by their fellow refugees to represent them. Their fares to Switzerland had been paid with the pennies contributed by refugees in the camps. Nevertheless, their arrival caused some surprise and—in the official Arab camp—dismay. The Commission and its staff, and the newspaper correspondents covering the conference, could not understand the appearance of a fifth Arab delegation, that of the refugees. As far as they could see, the Arab interest was amply represented by the delegations of Egypt, Jordan, Lebanon and Syria, particularly as these delegations were to all appearances holding out strongly for the refugees. They were soon to be disillusioned. As it turned out, the refugee group succeeded in establishing friendly contact with only one of the official delegations—that of Israel. The delegates of the Arab states would have nothing to do with them. Indeed, on one occasion, when the refugees tried to secure an interview with the Egyptian delegation, the Egyptians ejected them by force.

This incident called for explanation. It had made clear beyond doubt the hostility of the official Arab world toward the refugees. It was a bitter, active hostility, deriving as it did from a deep conflict of interest. Humanitarian considerations played no part whatever, even in those early days when care for the refugees had not yet been properly organized. This was explained to me with brutal frankness by an Egyptian delegate in one of our secret talks: "Last year thousands of people died of cholera in my country, and none of us cared. Why should we care about the refugees?" The only thing that counted was the political advantage which the Arab states could derive from the refugees *as refugees*. The Arab states not only had no interest in the repatriation or resettlement of the refugees; their interest required that the refugees should not be repatriated or resettled at all, or at any rate not for a long time, certainly not until they had ceased to be of political use. They pressed for the refugees' repatriation to Israel only because they knew this was not feasible in any case, at least not on any considerable scale. Israel's offer to repatriate a hundred thousand disconcerted them completely. They were left with no choice but to reject it, on the ostensible ground that it was not enough. As for the refugees' resettlement in Arab countries, which was part of the solution advocated by the General Assembly, the Arab Governments set their face against it from the start and have consistently to this day refused to co-operate in any scheme of the kind.

The Israeli delegation at Lausanne, on the other hand, quickly found common ground with the representatives of the refugees. Our basic interest was identical. Both groups were anxious to see a solution found soon for the refugee problem—the refugees themselves for obvious reasons, Israel on humanitarian grounds and, after the first days of Lausanne, to prevent the refugees from becoming a lethal weapon in the political armory of the Arabs. The ideas of Israel and the refugees on what the solution of the problem should be differed widely, but their common interest in seeing the problem solved was a fruitful basis for co-operation. Shunned and spurned by their fellow Arabs, the emissaries of the refugees maintained contact with the delegation of Israel during the whole of their stay at Lausanne.

Seeking a way out of the impasse created by the Arabs' demand for discussion of the refugee question alone and Israel's insistence that the question be studied in the framework of a general settlement, the Conciliation Commission switched to a new subject. Although the General Assembly's resolution had not made specific mention of the frontier problem, this was plainly a topic relevant to the conference. Eighteen months earlier, in its resolution of November 29, 1947, the General Assembly had defined the boundaries between the two states, one Jewish and one Arab, which were to come into being in Palestine on the termination of the British mandate. The Arab states had rejected this resolution and, when the mandate ended, invaded Israel in an attempt to prevent its implementation. As a result of the fighting and the Arabs' defeat, Israel found herself in possession of more territory than the General Assembly's original resolution had allotted her. The proposed Arab state did not come into existence at all, the greater part of Arab Palestine being annexed by Jordan.

The Arabs, having fought the partition resolution and the boundaries it laid down, could hardly now appear as their champion. But they saw that here was something of a stick with which to beat Israel. They did not want the establishment of an independent Arab state in Palestine as had originally been recommended by the General Assembly. They wanted themselves to annex as much of Israel as they could—at the very least those parts which lay outside the borders originally envisaged. If, on their submission, Israel had no right to these areas, they themselves had even less. But, at a conference never distinguished for its grasp of realities, they could ask for anything without a qualm and be sure of a patient hearing from the Commission, if not always from Israel.

The Commission, to contain the discussion within a frame of some kind, presented the delegations with the draft of a document, which was to become famous as the Lausanne Protocol. It appears occasionally even now in the repertoire of Arab propagandists. The Protocol read as follows:—

> The United Nations Conciliation Commission for Palestine, anxious to achieve as quickly as possible the objectives of the General Assembly resolution of 11 December 1948, regarding refugees, the respect for their rights and the preservation of their property, as well as territorial and other questions, has proposed to the delegations of the Arab States and to the delegation of Israel that the working document attached hereto be taken as a basis for discussions with the Commission.
>
> The interested delegations have accepted this proposal with the understanding that the exchange of views which will be carried on by the Commission with the two parties will bear upon the territorial adjustments necessary to the above-indicated objectives.

To this Protocol was attached (the "working document" mentioned in the text) the map of Palestine annexed to the General Assembly's resolution of November 29, 1947, showing the territory attributed to the Arab and Jewish states respectively. The Arabs would not sign the Protocol together with Israel. Two identical texts were accordingly prepared, and one each was signed, at separate meetings with the Conciliation Commission on May 12, 1949, by the Arab delegations and by the delegation of Israel.

The Protocol, like so much else at Lausanne, was a sham. The Commission must have known that it could not modify the declared policies of either party. But it was anxious to register a success of some kind, and the signing of identical documents by the two parties could be made to look like a step in the right direction.

The Arabs at once claimed that by signing this Protocol Israel had committed herself to acceptance of the partition frontiers. They have maintained this claim, *diminuendo,* ever since. In reality, neither Israel nor the Arabs ever accepted the Lausanne Protocol as anything but a basis for discussions with the Commission—*a* basis, it will be noted, not *the* basis. The exchange of views which the Commission was to carry on with the parties was to bear upon certain territorial adjustments. "Adjustment" is an elastic word. It can mean adjustment in any direction—increase or decrease—and was so understood, at least by the delegation of Israel.

Israel never committed herself to more than what the Protocol actually said. It empowered the Conciliation Commission to proceed with discussions on the basis referred to, without excluding any other possible basis. The two texts together constituted neither an agreement between Israel and the Arab states nor a commitment on the part of either to implement the General Assembly's resolutions of November 29, 1947, and December 11, 1948. By its legal nature each text of the Protocol was no more than a power of attorney, revocable at any time by the empowering party; it could also be renounced by the party empowered, the PCC. In 1950, Mr. Eli Palmer, then Acting Chairman of the Commission, informed the General Assembly that to his knowledge the Lausanne Protocol had not been implemented and that he doubted whether it could any longer serve as a basis for negotiation. The Protocol has never been invoked by the Conciliation Commission since 1951, but its soul goes marching on in periodical Arab attacks on the perfidy of Israel.

After Lausanne, the PCC went into a gradual decline. It has been moribund at least since 1951, when it reported to the sixth session of the General Assembly:

The Commission is of the opinion . . . that the present un-
willingness of the parties fully to implement the General
Assembly resolutions under which the Commission is operating, as well as the changes which have occurred in Palestine
during the past three years, have made it impossible for the
Commission to carry out its mandate.

In theory, however, the Commission still exists, and it has
from time to time shown a flicker of life. As late as 1957 it was
represented in Jerusalem by an official who conducted research
into questions of abandoned refugee property, mainly on the
basis of land registers and other cadastral material made available to him by the Israel Government.

But the Commission never revived after the failure of
Lausanne. In the summer of 1951 it invited the parties to a
further conference, at Paris, presenting them with what it
called a "comprehensive pattern of proposals." Israel stated
her willingness to subscribe to a declaration on the lines of the
preamble suggested by the Commission, in the following
terms:

> In accordance with the obligations of States Members of
> the United Nations and of signatories to Armistice Agree-
> ments, the Governments of Egypt, Jordan, Lebanon and Syria
> and the Government of Israel solemnly affirm their intention
> and undertake to settle all differences, present or future, solely
> by resort to pacific procedures, refraining from any use of
> force or acts of hostility, with full respect for the right of each
> party to security and freedom from fear of attack, and by
> these means to promote the return of peace in Palestine.

Israel subsequently went further and proposed that this
affirmation of pacific intent should take the form of a non-
aggression pact, to supplement the armistice agreements. But

the Arab states refused to give an undertaking along the lines suggested by the PCC. In the circumstances, the Commission was probably right in regarding consideration of a formal non-aggression pact as "premature." The Paris Conference never got beyond discussion of the preamble. It was this which convinced the Commission that it could not carry out its mandate.

It is idle now to speculate whether the composition of the PCC doomed it to failure from the outset. At the time of its appointment in December 1948, many people doubted whether a commission of three Powers with extensive interests of their own in the Middle East, and particularly in the Arab states, could achieve results. UNSCOP, in the previous year, had consisted of the representatives of eleven "small" nations which had no major interests in the region.

The true reason for the Commission's failure lay deeper. As time went on, the Arab attitude hardened. Not only did the Arab states refuse to recognize Israel or have dealings with her of any kind; they were now bent openly on Israel's destruction. In the face of such a policy, no conciliating agency could have much hope of success. If the PCC had adopted Dr. Bunche's procedures from the first and insisted on their acceptance by the parties, the chances of succeeding would have been brighter. At it was, it "never recovered from the loss of face inflicted on it by the Arab states."* The Arabs, without even having to go to the expense of paying the piper, had called the tune ever since the Beirut talks of March and April 1949.

One lesson, at least, is suggested by the experience of the PCC. As long as the Arab states are unwilling to negotiate with Israel directly, it is not likely that any indirect effort, be it "mediation" or "conciliation" or anything else, can succeed.

---

* *Israel and the United Nations* (New York, Carnegie Endowment for International Peace, 1956), p. 98.

The refusal to negotiate directly does not imply willingness to negotiate in any other way. The Arabs' refusal is absolute. It follows from their basic policy, which aims at the ruin and ultimate extirpation of Israel.

4

Jerusalem and the Holy Places

JERUSALEM, as George Adam Smith was not the first to observe, has none of the conditions of a great city. The whole plateau stands aloof, waterless, on the road to nowhere. "And yet," he continues, "it was here that She arose who, more than Athens and more than Rome, taught the nations civic justice, and gave her name to the ideal city men were ever striving to build on earth, to the City of God that shall one day descend from heaven—the New Jerusalem. For her builder was not Nature nor the wisdom of men, but on that secluded and barren site, the Word of God, by her prophets, laid her eternal foundations in righteousness, and reared her walls in her people's faith in God."

There was a problem of Jerusalem long before there was a problem of Palestine, in the modern sense. The so-called Status Quo, governing the Holy Places, was established in 1757 and publicly confirmed a century later by the Sultan Abdul Mejid,* but it did not put an end to disagreements— more between the Powers protecting different religious interests than between them and the Sultan. Palestine did not exist at that time as a political entity; it was divided among various vilayets of the Ottoman Empire, with Jerusalem and its environs forming a separate sanjak. The Moslem temporal power did not interfere in the management of the Holy Places. It kept a tolerant, unamused eye on the disputes between one religious group and another and was concerned mainly to avert serious breaches of the peace.

This system was maintained without essential change during the British successor regime after the First World War. If at first there was uneasiness in Catholic circles over the fact that a Protestant Power had secured control of the Holy City, as it turned out there was never any substantial cause for complaint. In those early years following the October

---

* In a firman of February 1852 addressed "to thee, my Vizier, Ahmed Pasha, Governor of Jerusalem, to thee, Cadi of Jerusalem, and to you, members of the Mejliss." This document treats of "the disputes which from time to time arise between the Greek and Latin nations respecting certain Holy Places which exist both within and without the City of Jerusalem." In essence it confirms existing rights. "You will take care," it concludes, "that henceforward my decision and my commands shall not in any way be contravened, either by those who profess the Greek, Armenian, Syrian and Copt religions, or by the Latins. You will take care to have the present Imperial edict recorded . . . to serve constantly and forever as a permanent rule. Understand this and give heed to the noble signature with which it is adorned." The Ottoman Government, as UNSCOP was to recall ninety-five years later, "possessed the police forces necessary to impose its decisions and generally to prevent religious disputes from resulting in religious strife."

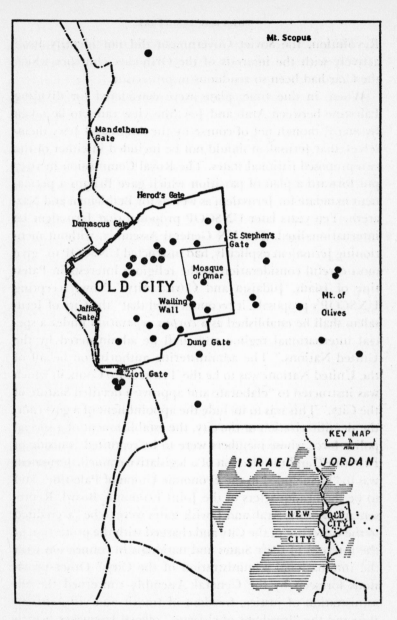

JERUSALEM, showing the Holy Places

67

Revolution, the Soviet Government did not identify itself actively with the interests of the Orthodox churches which the Czar had been so assiduous in protecting.

When, in due time, plans were considered for dividing Palestine between Arab and Jew, the view came to be taken by many, though not of course by the Arabs and Jews themselves, that Jerusalem should not be included in either of the two proposed national states. The Royal Commission in 1937 put forward a plan of partition which gave Britain a permanent mandate for Jerusalem as well as for Bethlehem and Nazareth. Ten years later UNSCOP proposed that Jerusalem be internationalized. The UN General Assembly, without mentioning Jerusalem explicitly, had instructed UNSCOP to "give most careful consideration to the religious interests in Palestine of Islam, Judaism and Christianity." Now, accepting UNSCOP's proposals, it recommended that "the City of Jerusalem shall be established as a *corpus separatum* under a special international regime and shall be administered by the United Nations." The administering authority on behalf of the United Nations was to be the Trusteeship Council, which was instructed to "elaborate and approve a detailed Statute of the City." This was to include the appointment of a governor, the demilitarization of the city, the establishment of a special police force whose members were to be recruited "outside of Palestine," and the election of a legislative council. Jerusalem was to "be included in the Economic Union of Palestine" and to be the headquarters of the Joint Economic Board. Representatives of the Arab and Jewish states were to be "accredited to the Governor of the City and charged with the protection of the interests of their States and nationals in connection with the international administration of the City." Other provisions foreseen by the General Assembly concerned the administration of justice, freedom of transit and visit, citizenship and the "freedoms of citizens," official languages (which were to be Arabic and Hebrew, but not precluding "the adoption of one or more additional working languages," as might be required) and, above all, the Holy Places. It was to be one of the "special objectives" of the Administering Authority

> to protect and to preserve the unique spiritual and religious interests located in the city of the three great monotheistic faiths throughout the world, Christian, Jewish and Moslem; to this end to ensure that order and peace, and especially religious peace, reign in Jerusalem.

The spokesmen of the Palestine Arabs and of the Arab states rejected the internationalization of Jerusalem outright. The Jewish Agency accepted it, albeit under protest. Internationalization formed an integral part of the partition plan, whose general advantages, notably the establishment of an independent Jewish state, outweighed the bitter sacrifice involved in relinquishing the ancient capital of Israel. In any event, the international regime was, by recommendation of the General Assembly, to remain in force in the first instance for a period not exceeding ten years. The whole scheme was then to be subject to re-examination by the Trusteeship Council "in the light of the experience acquired with its functioning," and the residents of Jerusalem were to be free "to express by means of a referendum their wishes as to possible modifications of the regime of the City." Since the population of Jerusalem in 1947 consisted of 100,000 Jews and 65,000 Arabs (of whom only slightly more than half were Moslems), the Jewish Agency looked forward with confidence to the outcome of the proposed referendum.

The General Assembly's proposals for the "special international regime" came to nothing. Like the rest of the partition plan, they were fought savagely by the Arabs. The Arabs succeeded in ruining the whole of the partition plan, except those parts of it which the Jews of Palestine implemented by themselves. In particular, the Arabs were intent on securing possession of Jerusalem, where they began by burning down a Jewish sector in the center of the city a few days after adoption of the General Assembly's resolution on November 29, 1947. Violence grew, and it was not long before Jewish Jerusalem was surrounded by Arab forces and placed under siege. The General Assembly twice passed resolutions for the "protection of the City of Jerusalem and its inhabitants"—to no avail. The Trusteeship Council as early as April 1948 abandoned the task of "elaborating" the special international regime; it was clearly impracticable under the circumstances. With the departure of the British on May 14, the city was invested by the regular armies of Egypt and Jordan. "As terrifying to-day as yesterday," a diarist wrote. "The distant boom, the fiendish whistle and crash, the echo of one shell hanging in the air with another already on its way, scattering death, injury, destruction. The whole city is the target; this sector, then that, then back to the first. Houses mutilated, streets strewn with scattered glass, torn telegraph wires, broken stones. What are they doing to Jerusalem!"* No one who lived through the siege of Jerusalem can forget it.

The people of Israel as a whole can never forget the siege—any more than they have been able, since the Babylonian exile, to forget Jerusalem itself. Having, as they see it, with their own forces alone saved Jerusalem from the Arab attempt to destroy it, they can never agree to see the city subject to a foreign, even if "international," regime. Despite all anxiety for the Holy Places, the United Nations and its members did

---

* Harry Levin, *Jerusalem Embattled*, a diary of the city under siege (London, Victor Gollancz, Ltd., 1950), p. 180. For another account of the siege, see Walter Lever, *Jerusalem is Called Liberty* (Jerusalem, Massadah, 1951).

nothing to protect Jerusalem, apart from passing resolutions. Israel resented this bitterly at the time and resents it to this day. The Jews of Jerusalem would not dream of relying for protection on an "international" governor and police.

This attitude, with which the official policy of the Israel Government conforms, has led Israel into conflict, or at least open disagreement, with other countries, and at times with the United Nations itself. The UN General Assembly is not in the habit of repealing or revising resolutions which have remained without effect, even if it is certain that effect can never be given to them. It has on record a large number of "Palestine resolutions" which contradict one another or have been rendered null by events. Very little pruning has ever taken place. It is many years since the General Assembly last discussed Jerusalem, and more than eight since it last adopted a resolution on the subject. But nominally it is still on record as favoring an international regime, and the Arabs have a convenient, if somewhat outworn, peg on which to hang their agitation.

There has, in fact, been a complete *volte-face* on the part of the Arabs. After rejecting internationalization outright, they have come to demand it. When Count Bernadotte suggested that Jerusalem become part of King Abdullah's domain, the Arabs accepted this "solution" with enthusiasm. But as soon as it became apparent that there was no chance of its adoption, they changed their tune. The armistice agreement between Israel and Jordan, based on the military situation at the time, drew the demarcation line through Jerusalem, leaving the "old" city in Jordan and the "new" in Israel. This is still the position today, confirmed implicitly by the Security Council's resolution of August 11, 1949. For the first time in centuries there has been an addition to Jerusalem's historic gates. Jaffa Gate, Damascus Gate, Herod's Gate, the Dung Gate, Zion Gate, St. Stephen's Gate—these ancient openings in the city wall have their modern counterpart in Mandelbaum Gate.* This is not, in fact, a gate at all, but the frontier point at which it is possible to cross the line between Israel and Jordan. It has become as celebrated as any of the old gates and carries more traffic than most. It is here, in no man's land, that the Israel-Jordan Mixed Armistice Commission meets in an abandoned Arab house. The only persons who, in principle, are not allowed to cross the line are Israelis and citizens of the Arab states. The "gate" is used regularly by consuls whose work takes them to both sides of Jerusalem, by United Nations personnel, by priests and members of religious orders and other "neutrals." The passage of tourists, free as far as Israel is concerned, is limited by Jordanian regulations, varying from time to time in accordance with political factors and security conditions. Over 88,000 persons crossed in 1956, and 73,000 in 1957.

In practice there is only one restriction on free access to the Holy Places. The Jordanian authorities do not allow Jews to go to the Wailing Wall, on the Jordanian side of Jerusalem. Jews had been free to worship at this most sacred of their shrines for almost two thousand years, from the destruction of the Temple to the year 1948. For the past decade this right has been denied them. There is no recorded instance of any Christian being refused access to any of the Holy Places of his faith, either in Israel or in Jordan. The fears which underlay the General Assembly's recommendations have in practice proved unfounded, except for the single instance of the Wailing Wall. Although the armistice agreement concedes in principle the right of worship at the Wall, the Jordanian Government has consistently refused to make it effective. If it were argued that an international regime would guarantee the Jewish worshiper his rights at the Wailing Wall, the answer must be that

---

* So called because it is adjacent to some houses built in the nineteenth century by a man named Mandelbaum.

this single consideration cannot outweigh its disadvantages and dangers. The rights exist, even if at present they cannot be exercised. The connection of Israel with Jerusalem predates even the Wailing Wall. It cannot be compromised for the sake of an immediate advantage.

It is this historic connection with David's City which made it unthinkable for Israel to establish her capital anywhere but in Jerusalem. Owing to the siege of Jerusalem and the rupture of communications, the administrative center of the new state was established in 1948 in Tel Aviv. But the Supreme Court of Israel had its seat at Jerusalem from the start. Israel's first President, Chaim Weizmann, was inducted into office in Jerusalem early in 1949, and the opening session of the Knesset was held there at the same time. The Knesset and most of the government offices moved to Jerusalem permanently at the end of 1949, shortly after the UN General Assembly had restated "its intention that Jerusalem should be placed under a permanent international regime."

By this resolution of December 9, 1949, the General Assembly requested the Trusteeship Council to complete the preparation of the Statute of Jerusalem, which it had interrupted in April of the year before, and enjoined it not to "allow any actions taken by any interested Government or Governments to divert it from adopting and implementing the Statute of Jerusalem." The reference to any interested Government "or Governments" arose from the fact that by this time Jordan too, deviating from general Arab policy, was objecting strongly to any idea of internationalization. Having secured, under the armistice agreement, *de facto* control of the "old" half of the city, she was not prepared to relinquish it in favor of an international regime. Although Jordanian Governments in recent years have made no statement on the subject, it is known that their policy regarding Jerusalem remains unchanged.

The Trusteeship Council did its utmost to carry out the General Assembly's directive. Meeting at Geneva in the early months of 1950, it devoted itself heart and soul to study of the question. On April 4 it completed a draft Statute but ultimately came to the conclusion that it could not be carried into effect and contented itself with a report to the Assembly. It had requested its President, M. Roger Garreau, to transmit the text of the Statute to the two Governments concerned. M. Garreau accepted in principle Israel's invitation to visit Jerusalem and discuss the problem on the spot, but when after repeated attempts he failed to secure a parallel invitation from Jordan, he abandoned his plan. "The results of the mission entrusted to me by the Trusteeship Council," he reported on June 1, "have proved disappointing, and the implementation of the Statute would seem to be seriously compromised under present conditions."

Israel had rejected the internationalization of Jerusalem, but she never denied the legitimacy of the world's interest in the Holy Places. In a memorandum submitted to the Trusteeship Council on May 26, 1950, the Israel Government offered "its full co-operation in seeking and implementing a solution of the Jerusalem question whereby the responsibility of the United Nations for the Holy Places may be reconciled with the freedom and independence of the City and its inhabitants." In detailing its own proposals, it declared that it regarded the consent of the people of Jerusalem as indispensable to the effective functioning of the city's institutions:

> The right of a mature population to select and maintain its own government cannot be challenged by any consistent adherent of democratic principles. Moreover, the preservation in Jerusalem of a regime based on the initiative and consent of its own population is not only an unassailable political ideal; it is also a dictate of practical statesmanship, with a

direct bearing on the issue of implementation. The idea that any regime for the protection of religious interests can endure amidst a discontented, aggrieved and turbulent population will be instantly rejected by any serious mind. Religious peace cannot be secured by political suppression.

At the time, Israel proposed what came to be known as "functional internationalization," as distinct from the "territorial" internationalization recommended originally by the General Assembly. She held that the legitimate interests of the world's religions could all be safeguarded by an international regime for *the Holy Places* in Jerusalem and did not require international government of *Jerusalem as a whole*. The safeguarding of Church interests in Rome did not require an international regime for the entire city with a denial of Italian sovereignty and democratic rights; it was enough to establish a special regime for the Vatican and St. Peter's and for a small number of other churches outside their precincts. Israel accordingly suggested the appointment of a United Nations representative, or "organ," to

carry out the following main functions in respect of the Holy Places in Jerusalem: viz., supervision of their protection; adjudication of disputes between communities as to their rights in the Holy Places; the maintenance of existing rights in connection with the Holy Places; the initiation of their repairs; assurance of their exemption from taxation; questions relating to the maintenance of free access subject to the requirements of public order; facilitation of pilgrimage movements; issuing of reports to the appropriate United Nations organs on all the above matters.

At the fifth session of the General Assembly, in the autumn of 1950, Sweden introduced a resolution drafted roughly along the lines of Israel's proposals. Despite the support of most Protestant countries, it failed to secure the necessary majority; combined Arab and Catholic opposition was too strong. On the other hand, a resolution moved at the same session by Belgium, reiterating the principle of a special international regime for Jerusalem, also failed to pass by the two-thirds majority required. The deadlock was complete. Never since has the General Assembly held a full-dress debate on the question of Jerusalem. Two years later, at the seventh session, the Philippine delegation unexpectedly sprang a motion reaffirming the principle of full internationalization; it was not adopted.

Israel never formally withdrew her proposal for "functional internationalization," but with the passage of time it has lapsed. Time, indeed, has shown that there is no need for special arrangements. During all these years there has been not a single complaint with regard to the security or accessibility of the Holy Places. Their legal status remains unchanged, they have been repaired whenever repairs have become necessary, they have been visited by tens of thousands of pilgrims from all over the world. Prelates from Catholic and Protestant countries alike have come to Jerusalem often and spontaneously expressed their satisfaction at the state of its religious sites. Access to the Holy Places is free and unhindered; their protection is assured. It is, indeed, doubtful whether in any previous age they have been regarded with the true reverence they inspire today. Disputes seem to be a thing of the past: there is no longer call for firmans or police. Jerusalem itself has remained essentially tranquil. The local commanders, Israeli and Jordanian, have direct telephone communication between them, with a view to spotting and stopping any incipient sign of trouble on either side. It is a tribute to the peacefulness of the city and its people that the line is seldom used. The fears felt ten years ago that with the passing of British rule there would be constant strife in the Holy City have proved completely unfounded.

One of the most curious aspects of the campaign for the internationalization of Jerusalem has never been adequately analyzed and perhaps defies analysis altogether. The campaign, in so far as it was conducted by religious interests, from the start fastened on Israel. All the pressure was brought on Israel. Israel alone was accused of "defying" the United Nations. The impression was fostered that the Christian Holy Places were in Israel, and that Israel was in some way heedless of world opinion in their regard. In fact, of the seven Holy Places recognized by the original Status Quo not one is in Israel territory. All are now in Jordan. A United Nations map issued in November 1949 shows the location of nearly forty sites in Jerusalem regarded as Holy Places in a wider sense. Of these only three are in Israel; all the rest are in the "old" city held by Jordan. It would have been reasonable to suppose that the brunt of world pressure would be directed against Jordan. Perhaps Jordan was wise to lie low and hold her peace when M. Garreau asked for an invitation to visit her side of Jerusalem. Israel, by taking an active part in the debate and by showing a willingness to meet world opinion as far as she could without sacrificing her position in Jerusalem and the rights of the city's people, may unwittingly have created the impression that this was a question that primarily concerned her, and not Jordan.

But the true explanation is probably different. After the failure of the Crusades, and specifically during the four hundred years of Ottoman rule from 1517 to 1917, the Christian world acquiesced in Moslem sovereignty over the Holy City. Despite the interval of thirty years of British administration thereafter, the idea of Moslem governance, as represented by Jordan, remained familiar and not wholly repugnant. There was no Christian protest against Count Bernadotte's proposal that Jerusalem be consigned to the temporal authority of a

Hashemite King. Jewish temporal rule, however, was a novelty. It upset accepted ideas. It seemed contrary to the preordained order. There may even have been a fear that Israel might extend her authority to the "old" city, where the Holy Places really are. Be this as it may, the prejudice against Israel's presence in Jerusalem persists in certain circles and influences the attitude of some countries toward Israel even in matters which have no connection with Jerusalem at all. No such difficulties have been raised with regard to Nazareth, which, also in Israel, has not been accorded specific mention by the United Nations since the General Assembly's resolution of December 11, 1948.

When the Knesset and the ministries moved to Jerusalem in December 1949, it was decided to leave behind in Tel Aviv the Ministry of Defense and the Ministry for Foreign Affairs—Defense on security grounds, Foreign Affairs for reasons of international comity. Almost the whole of the diplomatic corps was established in Tel Aviv; for the Foreign Ministry to put forty miles of mountain road between the corps and itself would cause inconvenience. It would, moreover, have been impossible, in a Jerusalem suddenly congested with ministries and their staffs, to find accommodation for all the diplomatic missions. But if the separation of Foreign Affairs from the diplomatic corps would have created practical difficulties of various kinds, it soon appeared that the Ministry's separation from the rest of the Government established in Jerusalem created constant difficulty too in the field of consultation and co-ordination. It was assumed that when the impracticability of a "permanent international regime" for Jerusalem was accepted by the United Nations, there would be no further objection to the transfer of the diplomatic corps.

A few months later the proposed internationalization of Jerusalem was, indeed, declared impracticable by the Trusteeship Council, but the Council's verdict was not accepted by the United Nations as such. Yet at its following session, the fifth, in the autumn of 1950, the General Assembly neither reaffirmed its former decision with regard to Jerusalem nor adopted any other. The issue was left hanging in the air. The Assembly did not even endorse the Trusteeship Council's expression of concern at the transfer of Israel government offices to Jerusalem. The transfer of the Ministry for Foreign Affairs now began to be canvassed, but nothing was done, despite criticism in the Knesset at the delay. When the sixth session of the General Assembly passed, in the autumn of 1951, without further discussion of the Jerusalem problem, the Government of Israel felt that it had allowed the United Nations quite ample time to make up its mind, and that it could no longer suffer the inconvenience of having the Foreign Ministry cut off from the Prime Minister and other government departments. Accordingly, on May 4, 1952, it announced that the Ministry would move to Jerusalem as soon as the necessary technical arrangements were completed. The seventh session of the General Assembly, in the autumn of 1952, passed like the fifth and sixth in 1950 and 1951 without any further decision on Jerusalem. Coming after the Government's announcement about the planned transfer of the Foreign Ministry, the Assembly's silence and inaction were taken to indicate acquiescence. Over three years had passed since the Assembly last pronounced itself on the subject of Jerusalem, and since the Trusteeship Council reported that internationalization could not be put into effect. By this time the Foreign Ministry's new buildings in Jerusalem had been made ready, and the move was carried out. On July 12, 1953, the Ministry completed its day's work normally in the old offices at Hakirya in Tel Aviv. The following morning it opened its doors in Jerusalem, to all intents as if it had been installed there always.

The move of the Foreign Ministry to Jerusalem was received

with enthusiasm by the Israeli public, which considered it long overdue, but by other governments and by the diplomatic corps with consternation bordering on anger. The Ministry had informed the diplomatic corps of the date of the move on July 10. Over a year before, the Government had officially announced its decision to transfer the Ministry to Jerusalem. When heads of missions had from time to time raised the matter, they had been informed plainly that the decision stood and that it would be carried into effect as soon as arrangements were ready for accommodating the Ministry and its staff of three hundred in Jerusalem. The fact that the buildings were going up and nearing completion was not a secret. They were plain for all to see, and the press had been reporting on their progress. The diplomatic corps could not fairly claim that it had been taken by surprise, though formal notice of the date was not given until late—for security reasons,* and to be spared last-minute protests which could not in any case have availed.

The sense of outrage with which other governments reacted took the Ministry by surprise. It had been thought that, when the first excitement died down, other governments would come to accept a situation they had long known must come about, particularly as they had only themselves to blame if five years of talk in the General Assembly had failed to produce an agreed solution. As for the practical difficulties, the Government was prepared to do all in its power to help the diplomatic missions find office and living quarters in Jerusalem.

Other governments, however, were not amused. Led by the United States and Great Britain, both of which themselves had voted *against* the General Assembly's last resolution on the internationalization of Jerusalem, they declared a boycott of the

---

* Many thousands of files and secret papers had to be convoyed to Jerusalem along the main highway, which for miles runs within a few hundred yards of Jordanian territory.

Foreign Ministry. They refused to allow members of their diplomatic staffs to visit the Ministry or even attend functions in Jerusalem unconnected with the Ministry. For a time, indeed, all visits to Jerusalem were barred, lest the appearance there of a diplomatic officer be interpreted as recognition of Israel's sovereignty or as acquiescence in the Foreign Ministry's move. This policy was without logic, since contact between the diplomatic corps and the ministries which had moved to Jerusalem three years earlier was normal, and heads of missions regularly called on the Prime Minister, who had been established there since the end of 1949. Some diplomatic missions went so far, on instructions from their governments, as not to address letters to the Foreign Ministry in Jerusalem. Letters were delivered at the small liaison office left behind by the Ministry in Tel Aviv for the transaction of routine business which did not warrant a forty-mile drive. The American Embassy in Israel to this day addresses all its communications, be they official notes or invitations to a cocktail party, in care of this liaison office at Tel Aviv.

A curious feature of this episode was the revelation, after the event, that the United States had been "on the point" of proposing a solution for the Jerusalem problem acceptable to Israel and other governments alike. The transfer of the Foreign Ministry had now made void a plan to which the State Department had been putting the finishing touches. If only Israel had not acted "precipitately," the Jerusalem issue would soon have been settled to everyone's satisfaction. It never, however, became known what the American plan was. Since it was no secret that the Foreign Ministry was about to move to Jerusalem, the authors of the plan might reasonably have taken the Israel Government into their confidence and suggested that the move be delayed a while until it could be carried out with universal consent. It is difficult to believe that such a request would have been rejected. As it was, Israel had had no inkling of any plan nor, indeed, any reason to suppose that after so many years of quiescence the Jerusalem issue was on the verge of again erupting into activity. There had been no intimation of the existence of an American plan until Israel was told that by her injudicious step she had killed it. This was the first but not the only time in the past ten years that Israel was to hear that by some action of hers she had nipped in the bud some happy solution which was on the point of being proposed.

The diplomatic ban could not be maintained rigidly for long. After all, the representatives of other countries were stationed in Israel to conduct business and cultivate relations with the Government. Gradually the boycott was relaxed, some countries allowing their heads of mission to visit the Foreign Minister, others deputing only subordinate officials to call at the Ministry. The practice of different missions varied, the government of each devising its adjustment to United Nations policy, to Arab pressure and to the realities of the situation. At one stage heads of diplomatic missions in Israel could be divided into four classes—those who were allowed by their governments to visit both the President and the Foreign Minister in Jerusalem, those who could visit the President but not the Foreign Minister, those who visited the Foreign Minister but not the President, and those who were forbidden to visit either. These varying codes of conduct would have caused more confusion than they did if the Israel Government had not been confident that everything would sort itself out in the end and maintained its position accordingly. The boycott of the Foreign Ministry has now long been a thing of the past, though almost all the embassies and legations remain in Tel Aviv. The only diplomatic missions resident in Jerusalem are those of the Netherlands, Greece, Guatemala and Uruguay. Cuba moved her legation to Jerusalem in the early summer of 1957 but after a few days found herself constrained, on American advice, to move it back to Tel Aviv.

A similar situation prevailed for a while over the presentation of letters of credence by the ambassadors and ministers of foreign states. Dr. Weizmann, the first President of Israel, resided at Rehovoth and received newly accredited heads of missions either at his home or in his office in nearby Tel Aviv. On his death in November 1952 he was succeeded by Mr. Yitzhak Ben-Zvi, a lifelong resident of Jerusalem, who soon transferred his office to the capital. The first diplomat to present his letters of credence to him there was the Netherlands minister, in May 1953, followed later in the year by the representatives of Chile and the Soviet Union.* The appointment of a new Italian minister, however, not long after the Foreign Ministry's move, created difficulties, as the Italian Government was unwilling to allow him to present his letters of credence in Jerusalem. After several weeks of negotiations it was agreed that the letters of credence could be presented elsewhere, but that the minister would present the customary *copie figurée* to the Foreign Minister, and thereafter be free to visit the Foreign Ministry, in Jerusalem. The ceremony was accordingly held at Tiberias, on the Sea of Galilee, where the President was taking a short rest. This was the last occasion on which letters of credence were presented outside Jerusalem; the date was December 16, 1953. The Government of Israel made it clear to other governments that it would from then on not accept ambassadors or ministers if they did not present

---

* The former before, and the latter after, the transfer of the Foreign Ministry. On April 17, 1950, the Soviet Union, which had voted *for* the General Assembly's resolution of December 9, 1949, informed the Secretary-General of the United Nations that in view of the opposition of the people of Jerusalem, Jews and Arabs alike, it was withdrawing its support of internationalization.

their credentials in the capital. The next minister due was the Swiss, who in April 1954 presented his letters of credence to the President in Jerusalem, despite much pressure on Berne from the Arab states, which tried to exploit the Italian precedent. As late as November 1954 the Arabs protested to the United States and Great Britain against the presentation of letters of credence by their ambassadors in Jerusalem, but by this time the matter had been settled for good. When the Italian minister was raised to the rank of ambassador in January 1956, neither the Italian Government nor, as far as is known, the Arab states demurred at his presentation to the President in Jerusalem. Tiberias belonged to a chapter which had been closed two years before.

By the time the Foreign Ministry moved to Jerusalem, concern for the Holy Places was no longer the factor which weighed mainly with other governments in determining their attitude. The Israel Government had from the beginning been scrupulous in its regard for the Holy Places situated in its territory, and it had indeed, in the note informing the diplomatic corps of the date of the Ministry's transfer, solemnly reaffirmed its policy concerning their preservation and freedom of access to them.* The Arab states, with the significant exception of Jordan, were now supporting internationalization of Jerusalem only because Israel opposed it, and it was above all a desire to placate them which at the time made most governments adopt the rigid attitude they did. The more limited a government's interests in the Arab states, the less doctrinaire it would be on the subject of Jerusalem. Other governments, even some which had themselves not supported internationalization, felt

---

* The note stated, *inter alia*, that the Government was satisfied that the location of the Foreign Ministry had no bearing whatsoever on the status of the Holy Places, "except inasmuch as the presence of the Ministry in Jerusalem is likely only to enhance the Government's capacity to discharge its responsibilities in respect of them."

Israeli delegates leave for Rhodes.

Egyptian delegates arrive at Rhodes.

A view of El Auja (Nitzana).

The Rhodes armistice plate.

"Armistice tent" on Tiberias–Damascus highway.

Work on the Jordan River development project
has been suspended since 1953.

Lake Huleh marshes.

Jerusalem:
Mount Zion and Old City Wall.

Christmas scene at Mandelbaum Gate:
checking passports.

The mouth of the Gulf of Aqaba:
blockaded by Egypt.

Eilat in 1950: blockaded by Egypt.

The blockade was lifted in 1956: Eilat begins to revive.

Home after three months in Egyptian jail.

UN observer inspects scene of "infiltrators'" raid.

Border police follow tracks of *fedayeen* after raid.

As Arab military threat increased, civilians
volunteered for defense duties in border zones:
Mr. Ben Gurion sets an example.

August 1948, at Tel Aviv: Stars and Stripes,
Hammer and Sickle flutter side by side.

Foreign Minister Golda Meir greets Kojo Botsio,
Commerce Minister of Ghana.

Foreign Minister Moshe Sharett welcomes
Prime Minister U Nu of Burma.

Representatives of
Zionist Organization
of America make
friends in kibbutz.

Ambassador McDonald after presenting letters of credence
to President Weizmann. On right, Mr. Ben Gurion.

The Chargé d'Affaires of Israel at Montevideo.

U Nu with Israeli children.

U Nu takes water
from Jordan.

President Ben-Zvi receives delegation from Ghana.

that as long as the General Assembly's resolution had not been repealed they could not recognize Jerusalem as Israel's capital. The fact that the General Assembly had had three years in which to modify its original decision or insist on its implementation, but had not done anything about it at all, was not regarded by these governments as relevant. The resolution was "on the books" of the General Assembly and must be regarded as valid, even if admittedly incapable of implementation.

For the past ten years an anomalous situation has existed with regard to the consular corps in Jerusalem. Since the rule of neither Israel nor Jordan in Jerusalem has been recognized except *de facto,* foreign governments have not allowed their consuls to present commissions on taking up their post. Since the government in whose territory consuls reside can issue its *exequatur* only at a consul's request and on presentation of his commission of appointment, all the consuls who have served in Jerusalem since 1948 have, with two exceptions,* been "unofficial" in the sense that, holding no *exequatur* from the Israel (or Jordan) Government, they cannot perform official functions which require recognition by the Government or its organs. No court of law, for example, need recognize a document validated by a consul who does not hold an *exequatur.*

The question of Jerusalem, which arose from the universal concern to safeguard the "unique spiritual and religious interests located in the city," thus degenerated for some years into squabbles of protocol and procedure. The Holy Places have been preserved, and, with the single exception of the Wailing Wall, access to them is free and secure. Israel has never denied the validity of world concern for their protection, but she cannot admit that this requires her to surrender

---

* The exceptions are the consul general of Ethiopia and the consul of El Salvador, both of whom requested and received the *exequatur* of the Israel Government. They are not accredited on the Jordanian side of Jerusalem.

Jerusalem to international rule. It would be an inconceivable affront to three thousand years of religious and national tradition to separate Jerusalem from Israel, or Israel from Jerusalem. Unless it be in response to Arab pressure, it is not likely that the attempt will again be made. If it should be, it would be bound to fail, as it did in 1948 and 1949.

5

Israel and Her Neighbors

THE ARABS have never left room for doubt about their hostility to Israel. The nature of this hostility and the forms it takes are less familiar. It has become a chronic disease of the body politic. Arab spokesmen maintain it can be cured only by the excision of Israel, which they are fond of calling a "cancer." Israel believes that the cure must be sought elsewhere. Psychotherapy could offer prospects—but before diagnosis can be attempted or treatment prescribed, it is essential to establish the symptoms.

After the failure of the "Mongolian massacre" in 1948,* the

---

* Azzam Pasha, then Secretary-General of the Arab League, said of the Arab armies' invasion of Israel: "This will be a war of extermination—a momentous slaughter which will be spoken of like the Mongolian massacre and the Crusades."

Arab states decided that for the time being they would have to carry on the war by other means. In any case, they were going to try—and see whether they succeeded. Success would depend largely on the tolerance of the rest of the world. The world, with honorable exceptions, did not disappoint them. The Arab "boycott," as it is euphemistically called, became a permanent feature of the international scene—an elemental fact of life, seemingly hopeless to resist. It penetrated every field of activity, the political, social, diplomatic, cultural and economic. Nowhere after Rhodes were the Arabs willing to meet Israel and talk with her, except in the Mixed Commissions set up under the armistice agreements, and there too, as time went on, mainly to spite her. They refused to honor other armistice obligations which involved meetings with Israel. Above all, they did not want other countries and other people to meet Israel and talk with her either.

The first step was the closing of the frontiers. This purpose was achieved automatically by making the armistice agreements permanent and refusing to move beyond them. The agreements forbade unauthorized crossing of the demarcation lines. All that had to be done was to refuse authority; Israel could have no complaint on this score. The only exceptions allowed were at Mandelbaum Gate in Jerusalem * and at Rosh Hanikra (Ras en-Nakoura) on the frontier between Israel and Lebanon—the former because of the peculiar situation in the Holy City, the latter, restricted to foreign diplomats and other very specially privileged persons, thanks only to the relative moderation of the Lebanese Government.

The closing of the frontiers found its counterpart in the treatment accorded to neutral travelers who wished to visit both Israel and one or more Arab countries. The Arab states began by refusing entry into their territories to anyone who

---

* See p. 72.

had visited or was planning to visit Israel, hoping in this way to discourage such visits or penalize "collaborators"; but they soon saw they were damaging only themselves. They accordingly modified their policy, while saving their self-respect, by refusing a visa to anyone who held a visa for Israel, in this way compelling travelers to resort to the subterfuge of two passports. Foreign governments, which could easily have insisted that the passports of their nationals were their property, and that it was the concern of no one else what visas appeared in them, acquiesced in this arrangement and regularly issued the two passports required. It was a device which of course deceived no one, since the presentation of a passport undefiled by a visa for Israel no longer proved that its holder had not visited or was not going to visit Israel with another passport carefully concealed in his pocket. At Mandelbaum Gate, indeed, the traveler who enters Jordan with a "clean" passport cannot possibly have come from anywhere except Israel. If he leaves Jordan without a visa for Israel in his passport, the frontier officials of course know that the visa is stamped in a second passport, which he will produce two hundred yards farther on. Syria recently discovered this flaw in the procedure. The occasional traveler who leaves Israel at Rosh Hanikra stows away his "Israel" passport and produces his clean "Arab" passport at the Lebanese checkpoint of Ras en-Nakoura. The Lebanese official rubber-stamps it in the usual way, showing that entry into Lebanon has been effected at "Poste Nakoura." When this passport is later shown at the Syrian border, it is rejected—because, although it bears no Israel visa, the imprint of "Poste Nakoura" proves that its bearer must have been in Israel before he entered Lebanon. The whole absurd game has now reached the point at which travelers, at least those who elect to cross at Nakoura and visit Damascus, have to equip themselves with three passports. They may have to have a whole library of passports some day, if other countries con-

tinue feebly to acquiesce in this practice which the Arab states
have forced on them. Folly of this kind is infectious and may
easily spread to other parts of the world.

The passport story would perhaps hardly be worth telling if
it were not a particularly bizarre illustration of the readiness
with which foreign governments have accommodated themselves to Arab measures against Israel. This readiness has extended, over the years, to far more serious matters. It has been
a factor in interstate relations with which Israel has had increasingly to contend. It is explained by the natural tendency
of governments, like commercial houses and private individuals, to keep out of the way of "trouble." They judge that the
Arab states, by their numerical superiority, can create more
trouble than a single Israel; and it is on this that the Arabs
rely. Having more oil and more people (thereby offering far
richer markets), and bestriding one of the most strategically
vital regions of the world, they reckon that other countries
must give in to their pressures—and usually their reckoning
has been correct. Israel calls it "appeasement." Other countries have seen it simply as the line of least resistance, not real-
izing until too late that they were inflating Arab bargaining
power to a point at which it has involved them in a degree of
trouble which they could have spared themselves by taking a
firmer line from the start.

The Arabs' economic boycott of Israel began, in primitive
form, on January 1, 1946. The Second World War was over,
the Arab states were members of the United Nations, the
struggle for an independent Jewish state had begun. By that
date, the Council of the Arab League had decided four weeks
earlier, each Arab state was "to take measures within the
framework of its constitution and laws, such as the withhold-
ing of import licences, to prevent the entry of Palestine Jewish products." The decision was loyally implemented, though

ingenious traders found loopholes in the various local enact-
ments and business continued on a limited scale. After the
establishment of Israel, the laws were tightened and penalties
increased. The Arab League established a Central Boycott
Office in Damascus, with branches throughout the Arab world
(notably at Cairo, Alexandria, Beirut, Baghdad, Tripoli in
Libya, Amman and Latakia). Large staffs were employed;
there was no end of comings and goings. The boycott tended
to develop into a private interest of the officials responsible
for its organization—in modern parlance, a "racket." Like
rackets elsewhere, it has been efficiently run. Since it is maintained in the name of the Arab national cause, it is practically
impossible for an Arab trader who does not wish to be ruined
to oppose or evade it. Only in Lebanon, a trading country par
excellence and the least fanatical of all the Arab states, has
criticism of the boycott offices appeared in the press.* One
such article, in February 1957, accused the boycott organizers
of having arrogated to themselves all three functions of government—the legislative, executive and judicial. It is not hard
to guess what malpractices must have occurred to evoke a complaint of this kind.

It was not long before the boycott was extended beyond the
Arab world. By 1950 measures were being enacted against foreign shipping. A black list was compiled of all ships known to
call at Israeli ports. Such ships were not to be allowed to trade
with Arab countries or to receive services in Arab harbors.
Shipping companies and their governments quickly adapted
themselves to these regulations, reserving certain vessels exclusively for the Israel run. There have been few exceptions—
mainly the occasional luxury cruiser whose valuable custom
Arab countries (particularly Lebanon) have not been willing

* Apart, of course, from criticism that the boycott organization was
not efficient enough. A patriotic editorial writer can always be sure of
earning applause for such a charge.

to forgo. If a freighter calling at an Arab port is found to be carrying goods consigned to Israel, the ship is black-listed and the goods are confiscated. This has become one of the accepted hazards of Middle East trading. The shipping boycott is to all intents complete, none of the interests involved having ever, despite their losses, thought it worth while to register more than a perfunctory protest. In particular, there has never been a unified protest by all the governments concerned. Goods might be confiscated in the Suez Canal, for example, one day from a Greek ship, another day from a Dutch, an Italian or a Norwegian. On each such occasion the government concerned might lodge a protest, but rarely more than halfhearted. Never have governments affected by these measures been willing to protest jointly or try to make their representations really effective. The boycott organizers soon understood that the maritime nations were ready, in practice, to bow to their regulations. This tame submission encouraged them to go out and seek new fields to conquer.

At one time Israel's international airport at Lod (Lydda) was well served by airlines operating to and from Asia and the Far East. It was possible to fly direct to Karachi, Calcutta, Colombo, Manila, Tokyo and other important centers—but the planes had to fly over Arab territory. It meant crossing either Saudi Arabia or Jordan and Iraq. These countries enacted regulations which forbade aircraft of any flag to fly over their territory bound to or from Israel. Saudi Arabia threatened that any such aircraft would be shot down. One by one the services were suspended—or rerouted through Cairo or Beirut, which thus benefited directly from the boycott. It did not matter that the regulations violated the Chicago Convention or the principles of the International Civil Aviation Organization, nor that Saudi Arabia was not equipped to carry out her threat. When Israel suggested to the companies and governments concerned that they should maintain their services through Lod and not give in to the new regulations, they admitted that the Arabs' action was illegal and a dangerous precedent—but it was accepted all the same. The reason given was that though no Arab country would dare, in practice, to shoot down a civil aircraft even if it could, the threat itself was enough to discourage passengers, and services through Lod to the Far East would no longer pay. For years there was no way of traveling from Israel to destinations east. The Suez Canal was barred, and there were no planes. The Arab boycott was able to chalk up another victory—a victory, once again, not against Israel alone, but against important foreign interests which had no direct concern with the Arab-Israel dispute. This particular boycott was broken only in 1956, when Air France introduced a service from Lod to Teheran, flying a roundabout route over Turkey, with connections at Teheran for Karachi and the Far East. In the following year this service was extended to provide direct flights from Lod as far as Tokyo, the plane still being routed, circuitously and uneconomically, to avoid the forbidden Arab zones.

On one occasion, in 1954, certain Arab states tried to go further, informing foreign airlines that in future they would have to choose between Israel and them. If a company used Lod, *all* of its planes would be barred from Arab airports. This was too much for the airlines and their governments. Energetic protests were made, with the result that within a week there came complete surrender. It was explained that it had all been a mistake—excess of zeal on the part of some subordinate official—and that there had never been any intention of placing such an alternative before the airlines. They apologized for the misunderstanding. In fact, this was a "try-on" by the Arab states. If it had succeeded in driving the airlines from Lod, the boycott would have scored another success. As in other cases, the first sign of objection on the part of its intended victims led to a swift retreat. There is little doubt that if other aspects of the boycott had been resisted as forcefully, the boycott could never have prospered in the way it has.

In the course of time the boycott was carried to other countries. Today it covers the entire world. As far as is known, no foreign government has yet allowed Arab boycott offices to be established openly in its territory, but in practice every Arab embassy, legation and consulate is a branch office of the central boycott organization. Diplomatic and consular representatives of Syria and Iraq have been particularly active in this field. Everywhere industrial and commercial concerns are bombarded with boycott propaganda. Foreign firms which do business with Israel, and especially those which have branches in Israel, are barred from Arab markets. Several large firms, yielding to boycott pressure, have given up their business with Israel or closed their factories there. Only the most stouthearted firms maintain their membership in chambers of commerce devoted to fostering trade with Israel. In many cases, the boycott has extended to Jewish firms in different parts of the world, firms which have no connection with Israel at all. Questionnaires have been circulated to thousands of firms, asking them for details not only of business connections with Israel, but of the religion or the racial origin of their principals. It is to the credit of several organizations, such as the Manufacturers' Association of Holland, that they have instructed their members to disregard questionnaires of this kind. (Needless to say, this has in no way diminished their trade with the Arab countries. It was merely another "try-on," and it failed.) An extreme example of boycott in another sphere is Saudi Arabia's insistence that there must be no Jewish officers or enlisted men among the American forces stationed at the Dhahran air base. The United States Government had no choice but to comply.

The boycott extends even to sports. By a decision of the Arab League in 1954, Arab participation in international sports and athletic events is encouraged, but only on condition that Arabs shall not compete against Israelis nor even against teams of other countries which include Jews. Israel has quite often had the benefit of "byes," sometimes up to the semi-final round, owing to the refusal of Arab teams to meet her.

There is, in fact, no limit to the Arab boycott, except the limit other countries are prepared to set it. There is little that Israel herself can do about it directly, though by its nature and extent it is a problem that occupies the Foreign Ministry all the time. The boycott will succeed as far as other countries allow it to succeed. It could not have succeeded at all beyond the primitive form it took in 1946, had it not been for the indifference or acquiescence of the rest of the world. At a time when discriminatory trade practices are generally frowned on, this extreme instance has been quietly accepted almost as a law of nature. It has been Israel's experience that to refer to it is to create embarrassment, annoyance and ill will. Foreign governments tend to be resentful if they are reminded of its existence and of their own surrender to it.

The history of the Arab boycott records one spectacular failure—the failure of the most ambitious "try-on" of all. In 1952 Israel negotiated a reparations agreement with the Federal Republic of Germany. As soon as it became known that Germany was preparing to negotiate, the Arabs began putting pressure on Bonn. Germany was threatened with all the fury of the boycott. The pressure grew heavier, and more desperate, at each successive stage. It started before negotiations opened, the Arabs attempting to prevent their being held at all. It continued throughout the negotiations, until the agreement was signed, releasing a veritable stream of Arab protest and threat. Pressure was now directed specifically against the Bundestag and the political parties, in an effort to prevent ratification. After the agreement was ratified in March 1953, the Arabs continued to do all in their power to hamper its implementation. At each stage, they sought to enlist the support of the German press, of powerful commercial interests, of leading industrialists, and some such support was indeed given them. But Government and Bundestag remained unmoved, and the bulk of public opinion, anxious not to identify itself with anything that savored of Nazism, stood firmly behind them. The Arab states, well represented at Bonn, tried their hardest, threatening to ban all trade with Germany—and even to break off diplomatic relations—if the agreement went through. Nothing availed them, despite a campaign which went on for years. The result was what Israel, in its communications to the West German Government, had predicted. Not a single one of the Arab threats was carried out. Diplomatic relations with Germany were not broken off. Trade between Germany and the Arab countries, far from being banned, has prospered.

GERMAN TRADE WITH THE ARAB LEAGUE STATES
(in million dollars)

Year	Imports	Exports
1950	59	29
1951	96	47
1952	110	70
1953	119	96
1954	155	110
1955	175	141
1956	194	153

It had been a case of the usual Arab tactics of trying to blackmail another country into compliance with the boycott. The campaign had been carried on with exceptional bitterness and vigor, originally on account of the large benefits that were to accrue to Israel, later also because it had become a matter of prestige. But essentially, like all Arab boycott pressure, it had been bluff. The Arabs had never had any intention of carrying out the least of their threats, and when their bluff was called they went about their affairs as usual, maintaining relations with Germany as if nothing had happened. From time to time their antireparations campaign still flares up, but, knowing that it has no chance of succeeding, they do not allow their grudge to spoil the business they do with the Federal Republic.

It would be wearisome to record all the instances in which the Arab states have sought to prevent other countries from establishing diplomatic relations or concluding commercial agreements with Israel. The pattern is always the same. In each case the Arabs make what they hope will be an effective threat. Almost anything is grist to the boycott mill. Once, learning that a certain country in Europe was planning to establish diplomatic relations with Israel, Egypt threatened to go back on a recent agreement to raise her diplomatic representation with that country from legation to embassy level. Not impressed, the Government concerned went ahead and entered into diplomatic relations with Israel. Exactly two weeks later, Egypt's legation in its capital became an embassy. But often Arab threats succeed, and Israel's relations with other countries have suffered as a result. Greece, for example, has refused Israel *de jure* recognition and insists on the device of "diplomatic representations" (instead of embassies or legations) in Jerusalem and Athens, because of her fears for the Greeks in Egypt. It has not availed her much. Since 1956 the Greek community there has been rapidly diminishing, and what is left of it has been impoverished, as a result of Egyptian legislation against foreigners.

Much of the Arab boycott of Israel has been on the border line between the political and the economic. It has sought to attain a political end—the destruction of Israel—by economic means. During the greater part of the first ten years, Arab leaders believed, or affected to believe, that Israel could be reduced to bankruptcy and ruin by being starved out—which meant not merely the denial of food and water to her people, though this was always a main objective, but her collapse as an economic unit. It is hard to say whether they still believe this, but they continue to act as if they did, and the boycott is maintained in all its rigor.

The Arab states rejected the scheme for a Jordan Valley Authority on the ground that it would benefit Israel as well as themselves, and because it envisaged the resettlement of up to 100,000 refugees in Jordan. They have always been peculiarly sensitive to projects calculated to develop Israel's water resources. In ten years Israel has been able to complete only one major water scheme—construction of the pipeline which carries water from the Yarkon River to the Negev. The Yarkon from its source to the sea is in Israel, and the pipeline runs through Israel territory for the whole of its length. The more ambitious Jordan River project has been shelved, and drainage of the Huleh swamps only just completed, owing to persistent sabotage by Syria. At one time Syria was studying a plan to divert the Jordan at one of its main sources, just inside her territory, and so prevent its flowing through Israel. She has been deterred, for the time being, only by the impracticability of the plan, not by the inhumanity of it, nor even by the knowledge that it would mean denying water to Jericho and the other districts of the Arab kingdom of Jordan through which the river flows in its lower reaches. The dominant idea, which overrides all others, is to damage Israel—in this case by robbing her of the water she needs for electric power, irrigation and food production.

The story of the Suez Canal blockade has become familiar as an aspect of the wider issue created by the canal's "nationalization" in the summer of 1956. For Israel, however, it is a major issue in itself. No Israeli ship has ever been allowed to pass through the Suez Canal. The rights of the matter are not seriously disputed, except by Egypt and the other Arab states. The Constantinople Convention of 1888 is quite explicit: passage must be allowed freely at all times, in war as in peace, to ships of every nation. Any exercise of the right of blockade is expressly ruled out. Egypt has pleaded that Article X of the Convention entitles her to deny passage to Israeli ships as a defensive measure, but Article XI makes it perfectly clear that measures taken in defense of Egypt cannot include denial of passage through the canal.*

After suffering this discrimination for three years, Israel laid a complaint before the Security Council, which on September 1, 1951, called upon Egypt to "terminate the restrictions," characterizing them as "an abuse of the exercise of the right of visit, seizure and search." The Council found that Egypt's practices could not be justified on the ground that they were necessary for self-defense and further noted that

the restrictions on the passage of goods through the Suez Canal to Israel ports are denying to nations at no time connected with the conflict in Palestine valuable supplies re-

---

* Article I: "The Suez Maritime Canal shall always be free and open, in time of war as in time of peace, to every vessel of commerce or of war, without distinction of flag. Consequently, the High Contracting Parties agree not in any way to interfere with the free use of the Canal, in time of war as in time of peace. The Canal shall never be subjected to the exercise of the right of blockade."

Article X: "The provisions of Articles IV, V, VII and VIII shall not interfere with the measures which His Majesty the Sultan and His Highness the Khedive . . . might find it necessary to take for securing by their own forces the defense of Egypt and the maintenance of public order. . . ."

Article XI: "The measures which shall be taken in the cases provided for by Articles IX and X of the present Treaty shall not interfere with the free use of the Canal. . . ."

quired for their economic reconstruction, and that these restrictions together with sanctions applied by Egypt to certain ships which have visited Israel ports represent unjustified interference with the rights of nations to navigate the seas and to trade freely with one another, including the Arab States and Israel.

Egyptian legislation had banned not only the passage of Israeli ships, but the carriage in other ships of specified goods, arbitrarily classed as "contraband," consigned to or from Israel. One of the main cargoes condemned as "contraband" was oil, ostensibly because it was a "war material," but in fact because it was vital to the maintenance of Israel's economy. It has been calculated that during the past ten years Israel has lost $100,000,000 through having to bring her oil all the way across the Atlantic from ports in the Western Hemisphere, instead of importing it from the nearby Persian Gulf, which Egypt's blockade measures made impossible.

Egypt paid no heed to the Security Council's order, although as a member of the United Nations she is bound, under Article 25 of the Charter, to accept and carry out the Council's decisions. Neither the Security Council nor any of the Great Powers or maritime nations did anything to induce—let alone compel—Egypt's compliance, and the subject soon became as great an embarrassment as the Arab boycott in its other manifestations.

Early in 1954 Israel turned again to the Security Council. By this time, with the Korean stalemate, the cold war was spreading to the Middle East, and the Soviet Union by its negative vote defeated a resolution which registered "grave concern" at Egypt's failure to comply with the Council's earlier order and which called upon Egypt "in accordance with its obligations under the Charter to comply therewith." Egypt, as was to be expected, did nothing of the kind, finding it easy to shelter behind the Soviet veto and the indifference of the other Powers. Great Britain was negotiating a new treaty with Egypt and preparing to withdraw her forces from the canal zone, and the United States was as anxious as she not to be embarrassed by the complication of Israel.

Israel waited six months and then sent one of her merchant ships, the *Bat Galim,* to pass through the canal from the Red Sea to the Mediterranean. The ship was detained as soon as she presented herself at the entrance to the canal. Her crew, brought ashore by force, were arrested on a trumped-up charge and thrown into prison. They remained there, without trial, for over three months. The *Bat Galim* herself and her cargo were confiscated. The Great Powers appeared to be less vexed with Egypt for this violation of Israel's rights than with Israel for provoking it.

There was nothing further Israel could do; it had become clear that she could expect redress neither from the Security Council nor by direct action. When, two years later, the Great Powers and other maritime nations saw themselves victimized by the highhandedness of Egypt's methods in the Suez Canal, they found their ability to defend their rights prejudiced by their own earlier failure to insist on respect for those of Israel. On October 13, 1956, the Security Council adopted a new resolution, embodying principles that should govern the management of the Suez Canal. The first of these was that there was to be "free and open transit through the Canal without discrimination, overt or covert." The resolution specified that this principle covered "both political and technical aspects." Egypt at once made it clear, and has repeated frequently since, that the rule could not apply to Israel, whose ships would continue to be refused passage.

Apart from the economic damage which Israel has suffered through Egypt's blockade measures, the most serious aspect of the matter has been Egypt's insistence on "belligerent rights."

Egypt has claimed that her armistice agreement with Israel, far from bringing the war to an end, explicitly confirms the continued existence of a state of war; and that she is consequently entitled to enjoy the rights, including the right of blockade, which are conferred on a belligerent by international law. The Security Council, in its resolution of September 1, 1951, had dealt faithfully with this claim, specifying that "neither party can reasonably assert that it is actively a belligerent or requires to exercise the right of visit, search and seizure for any legitimate purpose of self-defense." But Egypt, not heeding the other provisions of the resolution, did not accept this ruling either and has continued ever since to assert her belligerent status. In other words, she holds that one member of the United Nations can legitimately maintain a state of war against another. Here again the Powers and the United Nations have much with which to reproach themselves. They have never acted effectively in condemnation of this doctrine, and they may yet regret, in quite a different context, their failure to do so.

This is a crux of the Arab-Israel conflict. The Arabs maintain that the war has never ended and that, far from being under any obligation to end it, they are at liberty to pursue it by any means they have at their disposal and choose to use. They say this despite their insistence, in 1948, that they were not invading Israel to make war, but only by way of police action "to restore law and order."

For years Egypt applied blockade measures in the Gulf of Aqaba against ships bound for Israel's southern port at Eilat, whose development she succeeded in bringing to a virtual standstill. At the end of 1949 she set up guns at Sharm esh-Sheikh, commanding the straits at the mouth of the gulf. Unarmed merchant ships were fired on, stopped, searched and turned back. One or two tiny vessels managed to slip through under cover of night, or because they were mistakenly thought to be bound for the Jordanian port of Aqaba. But the evident dangers soon deterred owners and traders, and for years not a single ship called at Eilat.

When the Egyptian batteries were first installed at the entrance to the gulf, the United States inquired in Cairo about their purpose. The Egyptian Government, in an *aide-mémoire* dated January 28, 1950, replied that it had no intention of placing obstacles in the way of innocent passage through the straits: "consequently this passage, the only practical one, will remain free as in the past, in conformity with international practice and the recognized principles of international law." Despite this assurance, which at the time satisfied the American Government, as it was intended to do, Egypt maintained and intensified her blockade measures, ultimately refusing passage to all ships, wherever bound, which did not give advance notice of their intention to enter the gulf.

Egypt's blockade measures in the Gulf of Aqaba, like those in the Suez Canal, were debated in the Security Council. The Council's desire, in March 1954, to refer Israel's complaint in the first instance to the Israel-Egypt Mixed Armistice Commission was thwarted by a Soviet veto, and nothing was done. On November 3, 1956, after seven years of blockade, Israeli forces attained one of the main objects of the Sinai campaign. They captured Sharm esh-Sheikh, took the Egyptian garrison prisoner, spiked the guns and remained in occupation. The Gulf of Aqaba was thrown open freely to the shipping of all nations, and the port of Eilat began to revive. Four months later Israel withdrew her forces under United Nations pressure, but not before arrangements had been made for the UN Emergency Force to take their place and ensure that passage through the straits remained open. In the subsequent General Assembly debate it was clearly affirmed by the delegates of all countries except the Arabs and their allies that the Gulf of

Aqaba was an international waterway and that navigation in it was the free right of ships of every flag.

Egypt at this time, being still excluded from Sharm esh-Sheikh, was in no position to re-establish her blockade as she did in the Suez Canal, but she and the other Arab states maintained their claim that the Gulf of Aqaba was an "Arab sea" and that the right of navigating it was in their gift. Saudi Arabia, which holds the opposite shore of the gulf, and which in the meantime had garrisoned Aqaba itself, took over from Egypt the guardianship of Arab interests, protesting to all the world against the passage of ships to Eilat.

An unsavory aspect of this campaign was the introduction of a religious issue. Pointing to the Gulf of Aqaba as one of the traditional pilgrim routes to Mecca, Saudi Arabia claimed that the presence of Israeli ships contaminated it. As a matter of fact, Israel had more than once evinced her readiness to assist the pilgrim traffic in any way she could. It is ironical, in this context, that the only Moslems barred from the Mecca pilgrimage are the Arab citizens of Israel, whom Saudi Arabia refuses to admit.

The habit of violence spreads. Using force to maintain the boycott and blockade of Israel, the Arab states soon extended it to other fields. "Unauthorized crossing" of the armistice demarcation lines was at first confined to civilians. Arab villagers and refugees would cross into Israel, mainly at night, as marauders—stealing what they could, and carrying out a little sabotage or destruction on the side. They were a constant menace to the frontier villages in Israel, particularly, as happened more and more often, when they came armed. If they were detected and challenged, they would not hesitate to fire. At one time there was some sympathy with these "infiltrators," mainly outside Israel. They were thought to be mostly hapless refugees, unable to resist the temptation of gleaning what they could from fields which had once been theirs. There were undoubtedly such cases, but this was not a just view of "infiltration" as a whole, which came to be—like the boycott itself, though on a smaller scale—a racket carried on with the connivance of Arab frontier guards. Gangs were organized and armed; on their return there would be an "official" division of the spoils. From stealing and killing when cornered it was but a short step to setting out to kill—particularly when Arab leaders were calling loudly for "revenge," and when anyone who killed an Israeli was hailed as a patriot and hero. Israel for long bore this with patience, though patience was least evident in the border villages which were the nightly targets of "infiltrating" gangs. Still hoping for peace, the Government contented itself at first with protests to King Abdullah, from whose territory most of the marauders came. The King was told that the continuation of these raids must prejudice the prospects of agreement, and it is likely that he tried to stop them. But the gangs were not organized, at that time, by the central Government at Amman; they were the product of local initiative, and the more effective for that.

In the end, Israel had no alternative but to hit back. It will always be debated whether the means she chose were the best. They did not help her in the eyes of world opinion, which disliked "reprisals," especially when they appeared indiscriminate. But what was the alternative? Protest to the Mixed Armistice Commissions? This was done times without number, to no effect. All the Commissions could do was to establish guilt and censure the guilty. They could not take preventive or even deterrent action. The night after a Commission's meeting the raids would start again, setting off anew the futile round of accusation, investigation, discussion and censure. Might Israel not have complained to the Security Council? This was not possible over the heads of the Mixed Armistice Commissions and would in any case, as in so many other instances, have been fruitless. Nor was it possible to patrol or police every yard of a long demarcation line, much of it in difficult terrain. If "infiltration" could not be prevented, it must be attacked at its source—on the other side of the line. This was the inescapable conclusion, particularly after it became clear beyond a doubt that Israel was not merely troubled with isolated acts of lawlessness, but faced with an organized campaign. There was much pressure on the security authorities by the villagers themselves, who asked for nothing better than to be allowed to take the law into their own hands and attack their attackers. But the Government was never willing to countenance a "thieves in the night" policy. It saw itself responsible for security, and villagers in the border zones had every right to turn to it for protection. Any action that was decided upon would be taken by its own forces—it could not be left to the private initiative of the victims.

This was one of the aspects of the Israel Government's security policy which earned it the severest criticism abroad— that it used its regular armed forces to retaliate against "irregulars" or, more plainly, that the punishment was out of proportion to the crime. But it is doubtful whether any other government would, or could, have acted otherwise. Not many governments have, in our time, been confronted with a similar problem, on such a scale. The situation was not unlike that which long ago led to the outbreak of the Peloponnesian War. Where governments have had to deal with provocation of this kind, they have acted not very differently from the Government of Israel.* It was not until the attack on Kibya that con-

---

* The United States Government sent troops into Mexico on March 15, 1916, after the failure of all its other efforts to contain the marauders who harried the frontier zones. The American forces were not withdrawn till early the following year. On June 20, 1916, the Secretary of State, Robert Lansing, addressed a note to the Mexican Government: "It would be tedious to recount instance after instance, outrage

centrated action was taken against a marauders' base. This was in the night of October 14–15, 1953, after over four years of continual attack from Jordan. In the eyes of world opinion, four years of provocation counted for little against a few hours of military action. It was the military action itself which was condemned, all the more so for having led, contrary to intention, to the suffering of innocent people together with the guilty. Unhappily, women and children were killed. The fact that women and children had been killed by Jordanian "infiltrators" in Israel did little to relieve the impression, and

---

after outrage, atrocity after atrocity, to illustrate the true nature and extent of the widespread conditions of lawlessness and violence which have prevailed. During the past nine months in particular, the frontier of the United States along the lower Rio Grande has been thrown into a constant state of apprehension and turmoil because of frequent and sudden incursions into American territory and depredations and murders on American soil by Mexican bandits. . . . Representations were made to General Carranza, and he was emphatically requested to stop these reprehensible acts. . . . In the face of these depredations . . . , the perpetrators of which General Carranza was unable or possibly considered it inadvisable to apprehend and punish, the United States had no recourse other than to employ force to disperse the bands of Mexican outlaws who were with increasing boldness systematically raiding across the international boundary. . . . This Government has waited month after month for the consummation of its hope and expectation. . . . Obviously, if there is no means of reaching bands roving on Mexican territory and making sudden dashes at night into American territory, it is impossible to prevent such invasions unless the frontier is protected by a cordon of troops. No government could be expected to maintain a force of this strength along the boundary . . . for the purpose of resisting the onslaughts of a few bands of lawless men, especially when the neighboring state makes no effort to prevent these attacks. The most effective method of preventing raids of this nature, as past experience has fully demonstrated, is to visit punishment or destruction on the raiders. . . . The first duty of any Government [is] the protection of life and property. This is the paramount obligation for which governments are instituted, and governments neglecting or failing to perform it are not worthy of the name."

there was never a second Kibya. Care was taken later to attack only police forts, military posts and other such bases from which the raiders operated. The Security Council expressed the "strongest censure" of the Kibya action, at the same time requesting the Government of Jordan to "continue and strengthen" its measures against "crossing of the demarcation line by unauthorized persons often resulting in acts of violence."

Throughout the following years of attack and counterattack on the frontier, the Israel Government prided itself on never initiating action against an Arab state. In every case Israeli action, punitive rather than retaliatory, came after a particularly brutal murder or a series of exceptionally destructive raids. Israel's attitude will seem disingenuous only to those who have never lived under constant guerrilla assault or cannot imagine what it is like. The Government's policy did nothing to ease Israel's international position, but this could not be the primary consideration. It was the Government's first duty to afford its own citizens what protection it could, by whatever means it judged most effective. The rising toll of dead and wounded, and the strain on the population, particularly in the border regions, made action unavoidable. If the Government had not taken the responsibility on itself, there would have been "private" action with far more unpleasant results.

Defenders of the Kibya operation claimed that it was effective, by compelling the Jordanian authorities to take stronger measures against "infiltrators." The number of Israelis killed in the areas bordering on Jordan had been growing: eleven in 1949, eighteen in 1950, forty-four in 1951, forty-six in 1952, fifty-seven in 1953. After Kibya it dropped to thirty-four in 1954, eleven in 1955, rising again (to seventy-four in 1956, when Egypt operated *fedayeen* raiders from Jordanian territory. Be this as it may, the losses suffered by Israel were severe, warranting all the anxiety the Government felt. Up to the time of the Sinai campaign there were something like 11,650 "incidents," in which 434 Israelis were killed and 942 wounded by Arab raiders. Of these "incidents," about 7,850 were the work of "infiltrators" from Jordan, some 3000 from Egypt, 600 from Syria and 200 from Lebanon.* "Incidents" included train wrecking, sniping, the blowing up of houses and water installations, attacks on road transport, theft of water pipes and crops, mining of tracks and other forms of sabotage, in addition to much killing in cold blood. During most of 1956, a fair number of "incidents" which originated in other countries, particularly in Jordan and Lebanon, were in fact the work of *fedayeen* operating under Egyptian orders. The extent of Egyptian responsibility is accordingly larger than appears from these figures, but this responsibility should not be measured by arithmetic alone. Throughout the eight years which preceded the Sinai campaign, much of the political inspiration and incitement came from Egypt, reaching new heights after the rise to power of Gamel Abdul Nasser. It was Egypt, too, which introduced refinements such as plastic mines and organized the *fedayeen* as full-blown military units. By 1956 the *fedayeen* campaign, launched from bases in Gaza and Sinai, had attained proportions which made a major counter-

---

* The relatively small number of "incidents" on the Lebanese border was due to Lebanon's desire for a quiet life. Much of the little trouble that occurred arose from ordinary petty crime or the smuggling which is endemic along land frontiers in most parts of the world. In the eight years from the signing of the armistice to the spring of 1957 only seven Israelis lost their lives in this area. Seriously embarrassed when Egyptian-trained *fedayeen* began using its territory as a base of operations against Israel, the Lebanese Government showed surprising efficiency in suppressing them. It is a common sight to see Israel and Lebanon farmers working within a few yards of one another on either side of the border. Had Egypt and Jordan shown as peaceable a disposition, most of the strife on their borders could have been averted.

move essential. Instead of dealing with the problem piecemeal, Israel determined to wipe out the bases and rout the men who operated from them. This was one of the two major objects of the Sinai campaign, which in five days drove the Egyptian army, *fedayeen* and all, back beyond the Suez Canal. It did not make Egypt any better disposed toward Israel, but it put an end to the guerrilla raids which had been harassing the border zones. For the first time in years villagers were able to sleep at night, instead of piling watch duty on the exhaustions of a working day.

The Arab campaign against Israel has been conducted on every front for the past ten years with a vigor and fixity of purpose that might have been devoted to a better cause. The very intransigence of Arab policy has daunted the world. Little effort has been made to curb it. From time to time, self-appointed emissaries of good will have journeyed between Jerusalem and Cairo, trying to see what they could do. On rare occasions, the official representative of some influential third party has been sent on such a mission, always welcomed gratefully by the Israel Government, and as often returning empty-handed and disillusioned from Egypt. Since the death of King Abdullah, no Arab ruler has been willing to parley with Israel. The fact that the Arab states put themselves in the wrong by refusing to negotiate with Israel has not weighed with them. They do not recognize Israel; consequently there is no one with whom to negotiate. Their whole attitude is based on the thesis that Israel has no right to exist and that to negotiate with her is out of the question because it would mean conceding her this right.

Only once since the fiasco of Lausanne has a concerted effort been made by other countries to induce the Arabs to negotiate. At the seventh session of the UN General Assembly in 1952 eight delegations* presented a resolution which, reaffirming the principle that the Arab states and Israel "have the primary responsibility for reaching a settlement of their outstanding differences," urged "the Governments concerned to enter at an early date, without prejudice to their respective rights and claims, into direct negotiations for the establishment of such a settlement, bearing in mind the resolutions as well as the principal objectives of the United Nations on the Palestine question, including the religious interests of third parties."

One might have thought that from any viewpoint of international comity, and from that of the United Nations itself, the wording of this resolution was unexceptionable. But no sooner was it put forward than the Arabs raised an outcry, claiming that they were being made the victims of a political maneuver. They fought the resolution tooth and nail, but it was adopted by the *ad hoc* Political Committee of the Assembly by thirty-two votes against thirteen, with thirteen abstentions. The thirteen negative votes were cast by the Arab states and by other "Afro-Asian" nations, which at that time were feeling their way as a bloc. The abstainers were a mixed bag—mainly the Soviet Union and its supporters, and a few Latin American and other Catholic countries. The Arabs redoubled their efforts in the week that passed between the recommendation of the *ad hoc* Committee and the decisive vote in the plenary session of the General Assembly itself. The Soviet bloc and some Latin American abstainers joined the Arab camp, while other Latin Americans switched from support to abstention. When it came to a vote, only twenty-four countries supported the resolution, those who opposed it were now twenty-one, and fifteen abstained. Failing to obtain a two-thirds majority,

* Canada, Cuba, Denmark, Ecuador, the Netherlands, Norway, Panama, Uruguay—none with extensive interests in the Middle East and all strictly neutral in the Arab-Israel dispute.

the resolution was not adopted. Thus ended the only real effort ever made to put the weight of the United Nations behind the demand for direct negotiations between the Arab states and Israel. In later years, as Soviet support for every Arab thesis became all but automatic, and the Asian-African bloc grew in numbers and strength, any prospect of the General Assembly's adopting such a resolution vanished altogether. The United Nations was unable to command obedience to its own most elementary principles, of which the settlement of disputes by peaceful means is the first.

The Arabs could not be blamed for concluding that the world was not seriously interested in peace between them and Israel. The world would no doubt have liked to see peace come about, by a parthenogenetic process of some kind, but it was not prepared to exert itself for it. Twenty-one countries actually voted against this 1952 effort to bring the two sides together, and fifteen did not feel strongly enough about it to commit themselves one way or the other. The Arabs could not help seeing this as license to continue on the path of intransigence.

In the circumstances, there has been nothing to induce the Arabs to make peace. Peace could not pay them as long as the United Nations was not even prepared to adopt a resolution commending it. Even the defeated resolution had not ventured to pronounce the word "peace"; it had relied on the old evasion of "settling outstanding differences." The world hoped everything would right itself in time. Preoccupied with the graver crisis in Korea, it adopted an attitude of laissez faire regarding the Middle East. Within little more than a year, as Korea receded into the background and active power rivalries shifted nearer to the scene of the Arab-Israel conflict, it had become too late to do anything effective. By January 1954 the Soviet Union was vetoing resolutions which were not to the Arabs' taste. In the following year, with other Communist states, it began openly to espouse the Arab cause and supply Egypt with arms.

In their attitude toward peace with Israel, the Arab states naturally consulted their own interests. They were left to make the reckoning between Israel and themselves, since the rest of the world was content to stand aside and let matters take their course. What advantages could peace with Israel bring them? A settlement of the refugee problem? In this they were not interested. Direct land communication across Israel between Cairo and Beirut, or Cairo and Amman? This would doubtless be a convenience, but only for the privileged few who traveled at all and preferred to do their traveling by rail or road. As long as there were sea and air communications, the overland route could be dispensed with. The prospects of trade with Israel were not attractive enough to weight the scales for peace. There was nothing else.

On the other hand, by maintaining a state of near-war and tension, the Arab world reaped obvious advantages. It provided itself with a grievance it could nurse to its heart's content —and in politics there are few assets more valuable than a grievance. It focused international attention on itself, by becoming a power for mischief; and it reckoned that, like any group which made enough of a nuisance of itself, it might hope for the prizes of appeasement. Seeing as early as 1949, and even before, that this hope would not be disappointed, it felt encouraged to persist. Domestically, hostility to Israel promised rich rewards. There was nothing like a bitter harangue against Israel to rouse the masses and divert their minds from less appealing topics. The Arab League, as such, has been held together to this day largely by the boycott and other common action against Israel. With the growing clash of interests between the Arab states themselves, the Arab League clings to Israel as its main *raison d'être*. It is not cynicism to say that if Israel did not exist, the Arabs would have to invent her.

Faced with this situation, Israel is bound to ask herself what she can do, or what more she could have done, to overcome the Arabs' hostility. True, the roots of Arab resentment go back nearly forty years to the birth of the British mandate. But deep-rooted hostility can be, and has been, overcome, as the experience of other countries has shown. The official leadership of the Palestine Arabs never reconciled itself to the Jewish National Home, let alone the notion of a Jewish state. But Jews and Arabs co-operated in trade, in local government, as civil servants, and in a multitude of other fields. When the Jewish Agency in 1947 agreed to the partition plan, which would have left in Israel's territory almost as many Arabs as Jews, it knew it could not escape grave difficulties in practice, but it was prepared to establish a fully democratic state and accept the Arabs as equal citizens. As soon as the General Assembly's resolution was adopted, the Jewish Agency declared its policy anew and called for the good will of the Arab world. Even after six months of Arab violence had betokened the very opposite of good will, the authors of the Declaration of Independence adopted by Israel on May 14, 1948, were not too disillusioned to proclaim:

> In the midst of wanton aggression, we yet call upon the Arab inhabitants of the State of Israel to preserve the ways of peace and play their part in the development of the State, on the basis of full and equal citizenship and due representation in all its bodies and institutions, provisional and permanent.
>
> We extend our hand in peace and neighborliness to all the neighboring states and their people, and invite them to co-operate with the independent Jewish nation for the common good of all.

On August 1, 1948, after establishment of the "permanent" truce, Israel made the first of her many peace offers. They were to be repeated time and again, whenever the occasion appeared favorable. It was, in fact, a standing offer, and it stands to this day. After the armistice agreements were signed, Israel followed up her general peace offer with more specific action and proposals. She carried into effect the "reunion of families" scheme, undertook to pay compensation for abandoned Arab lands, agreed to the return of 100,000 refugees, released "frozen" Arab bank accounts, resettled some 35,000 refugees in her own territory, offered Jordan a free zone in Haifa port. Not a single conciliatory move came from the Arab side. One can keep one's hand stretched out for quite a long while, as Mr. Sharett said at the time, but, if no one takes it, in the end it is bound to drop. Disillusion set in, and domestic critics began charging the Government with appeasement. The more offers were made, the more the Arabs expected and were willing to accept, without showing the slightest sign of accepting Israel herself. This was not a process that could go on forever, but it was renewed from time to time. At the seventh session of the General Assembly, in 1952, Israel put forward a detailed "blueprint for peace,"* only to see it rejected out of hand by the Arabs. The only progress Israel was ever able to make was with King Abdullah, who sincerely desired peace. His death came at a time when powerful forces in the Arab world and in his own country were frustrating all hope. The manner of it did not encourage other Arab leaders to follow his example. When, years later, Mr. Ben Gurion offered to meet Colonel Abdul Nasser to talk things over, there was no response— though the offer was perfectly sincere and the idea itself undeniably sound at a time when the Prime Ministers of Pakistan and India could meet to discuss Kashmir and President Eisenhower and Marshal Bulganin came together at their "summit."

---

* Reproduced in full in Abba Eban's *Voice of Israel* (New York, Horizon Press, 1957), pp. 93–122.

What Israel could never do—indeed, what no country could have done—was to accept Arab demands in advance of negotiations. From time to time Arab spokesmen have said that they might be willing to talk (never "to make peace") with Israel if first she fulfilled certain conditions. Such a condition might be, at one time, that Israel agree to the repatriation of all the Arab refugees; at another, that she surrender territory. No such "offer" was ever intended seriously. The Arabs demanded the impossible precisely because they knew it was impossible and could not conceivably lead to negotiations. Even if it had been intended seriously, Israel could not have accepted it. No country in its senses will make concessions *before* it negotiates, however willing it may be—and Israel always was willing—to make concessions to the other side in the course of negotiations. The Arabs were merely trying to create a good impression at times when it suited them, and to see whether they could wheedle some major concession out of Israel after the manner of the released bank accounts and the reunion of families—without giving anything in return. Israel *could,* of course, appease the Arabs, by crippling and ultimately liquidating herself, giving away a piece of territory here and some economic titbit there, until there was nothing left. But this is not a course that could commend itself to her or should commend itself to anyone else. At a critical stage of Israel's history, on May 26, 1948, when the Arabs rejected the Security Council's call for a cease-fire and demanded that Israel's statehood be abrogated and the Israeli forces disarmed, Mr. Abba Eban addressed the Security Council: "If the Arab states want peace with Israel, they can have it. If they want war, they can have that too. But whether they want peace or war, they can have it only with the State of Israel."*

This remains the central point. As long as the Arab states

---

* Abba Eban, *op. cit.,* p. 16.

are not willing to recognize Israel and Israel's right to exist, there can be no hope of peace, nor even of "settling outstanding problems." The current international situation, with its interplay of mighty forces, offers no prospect of the Arabs' changing their attitude—nor any reason, from their point of view, why they should. The Arab world is passing through a crisis which is racking it socially, morally and politically. When this crisis is resolved, a new Arab world will emerge. It is impossible to predict its character or aspirations, but if they are not compatible with peace with Israel, peace cannot come in our time. Israel has shown that she could ride out ten years of unrelenting enmity from the Arab side, and she can live with it for decades and generations more if she must. She has won a foothold in world markets which she would never have explored if the Arab countries had been open to her commerce. She has welded a million new immigrants into a united people much faster than she could have done but for their consciousness of a common danger. The situation has not been without its incidental advantages for Israel. But all this is cold comfort. Israel would always have preferred, and would still prefer, peace with her neighbors; and she would do almost anything to attain it—short of doing away with herself.

6

The Arab Refugees

IN THE LATE AUTUMN of 1956 a British newspaper correspondent was discussing Iraq's development plans with an Iraqi
Cabinet Minister at Baghdad. The Minister lamented Iraq's
shortage of manpower. "Why don't you bring over the Arab
refugees from Palestine?," inquired the correspondent. "Oh,
we couldn't do that," the Minister replied. "That would solve
the refugee problem!"

The story may sound tendentious but it is perfectly true—
and the Iraqi Minister was speaking the truth. Resettlement of
the Arab refugees in Iraq *could* solve the refugee problem—
and incidentally one of Iraq's own development problems. But
it has never been a feasible solution since the Arab states for

their own political ends have been determined to keep the refugees as refugees. The official news commentator of Cairo Radio, reacting to a statement by Mr. Ben Gurion in July 1957, made their attitude quite clear: "The fact that Israel is trying to solve the refugee problem proves that she has an interest in its solution. This alone is enough to damn any such attempt in Arab eyes."

For long, the fundamental truths of the refugee situation were glossed over or concealed, especially in United Nations reports. Though they have been known and acknowledged at least since Lausanne, it was years before they were spoken of publicly. Congressmen Smith and Prouty broke the spell of silence when they reported in 1954: "It is necessary to induce a desire on the part of the Arabs to work out a solution to the [refugee] problem. Such a desire does not exist at present."* In May 1957 a conference of seventy-two international organizations, concerned with refugee problems in general, met at Geneva. Dr. Elfan Rees, Adviser on Refugees to the World Council of Churches, pointed out that "political issues aside, the Arab refugee problem is by far the easiest postwar refugee problem to solve by integration" (that is, as opposed to the two other "classic solutions" of repatriation and emigration). Dr. Rees went on to explain that the refugees were "by faith, by language, by race and by social organization . . . indistinguishable from their fellows of their host countries" (that is, the Arab states), that there was room and land for them there, and that, "more unusually still," there was the money to make their integration possible—the $200,000,000 voted for this purpose by the UN General Assembly at its sixth session,

* *The Arab Refugees and Other Problems in the Near East,* Report of the Special Study Mission to the Near East comprising Hon. Lawrence H. Smith and Hon. Winston L. Prouty, of the House of Representatives Committee on Foreign Affairs (Washington, United States Government Printing Office, 1954), p. 5.

which "remains unspent . . . simply for political reasons."

"Political issues aside . . . simply for political reasons"—here, alas! is the rub. The Geneva conference declared itself "well aware that an equitable solution can only be arrived at by political action." Dr. Rees had of course used the word "simply" as a colloquialism. Like everyone else, he knew that the matter was far from simple. It is, in fact, wholly a political problem; had the Arab states seen it as a humanitarian problem, they could not have hardened their hearts all these years. The Geneva conference made no very revolutionary discovery. It had long been evident that everything depended on a political decision by the Arab states.*

The flight of the refugees began suddenly, at Tiberias, on the night of April 18, 1948, four weeks before the end of the British mandate. In a single night the entire Arab population of Tiberias—six thousand men, women and children—disappeared across the frontiers of Syria and Jordan. It was a cataclysmic event. I vividly recall the news reaching Jerusalem early next afternoon. It was not believed. No one could under-

---

* Dr. Rees's statement is too long to be reproduced here in full. It is an expert's analysis of the situation: "The Arab refugees and the Arab states claim that there can be only one solution to this particular problem, the solution of repatriation. It is, however, a fact that repatriation has never yet proved to be a solution to any modern refugee problem. . . . Apart from the historical breakdown of such solutions, I am bound to say that, given the fact of the existence of the State of Israel and its present density of population, the repatriation of a million Arab refugees seems to me to be physically and politically impossible. . . . Integration is the one hope of the Arab refugees from Palestine. We must recognize that the bar to that solution is a purely political bar. While we are not here to deal with politics, we can surely express our concern that these refugees cannot remain indefinitely suspended in some international limbo." The text of the statement is reproduced *in extenso* in *Christian News from Israel*, VIII, No. 1–2 (June 1957), pp. 36–41.

stand what had happened, or how. How could all these people, ordinary folk, almost a thousand families, rich and poor, old and young, have packed their chattels and taken themselves off into the night? Someone had organized it—but who, and why? Our first reaction was one of dismay, as we found ourselves in the presence of a phenomenon we could not explain. The Deir Yassin killings of a week before were no explanation. Tiberias was at the other end of the country. The panic spread, and within a few days the sixty-five thousand Arabs of Haifa had fled, followed by the fifty thousand of Jaffa. Only in the Jerusalem area, where Deir Yassin lay, did the Arab National Committee threaten action against runaways—without success. The mystery deepened. A contemporary diary* records the bewilderment of the Jews:

> Extraordinary news from Tiberias . . . I wonder what's behind it. It can't just be fear of the Jews . . .
> There is something eerie in the way the Arabs are running. . . . Some unseen hand is stimulating this exodus, first in Tiberias, now Haifa . . .
> It remains a puzzle.

The departure of the Arabs was inexplicable, but the Jews were certain it could bode no good and at first strove to arrest it. The flight from Tiberias was so sudden that nothing could be done to stop it. But at Haifa, a few days later, the first astonishment had worn off, and on April 26 and 28 a high-ranking British officer reported to Police Headquarters in Jerusalem:

> Every effort is being made by the Jews to persuade the Arab population to stay and carry on with their normal lives, to

---

* Harry Levin, *Jerusalem Embattled* (London, Victor Gollancz, Ltd., 1950), pp. 81, 90, 104.

get their shops and businesses open and to be assured that their lives and interests will be safe . . .

The Jews are still making every effort to persuade the Arab population to remain and settle back to their normal lives in the town.*

The *Economist* of October 2, 1948, carried the report of a British eyewitness:

During subsequent days the Jewish authorities . . . urged all Arabs to remain in Haifa and guaranteed them protection and security. As far as I know, most of the British civilian residents whose advice was asked by Arab friends told the latter that they would be wise to stay. However . . . various factors influenced their decision to seek safety in flight. There is but little doubt that the most potent of these factors were the announcements made over the air by the Arab Higher Executive, urging all Arabs in Haifa to quit. The reason given was that upon the final withdrawal of the British, the combined armies of the Arab States would invade Palestine and "drive the Jews into the sea," and it was clearly intimated that those Arabs who remained in Haifa and accepted Jewish protection would be regarded as renegades.

On August 16, 1948, in the course of an interview he gave to the Lebanese newspaper *Sada al-Janub*, Mgr. George Hakim, Greek Catholic Archbishop of Galilee, himself an Arab of Egyptian origin, said:

The refugees had been confident that their absence from Palestine would not last long, that they would return within

---

* *Cf.* Moshe Pearlman, *The Army of Israel* (New York, Philosophical Library, 1950), p. 116.

a few days—within a week or two. Their leaders had promised them that the Arab armies would crush the "Zionist gangs" very quickly and that there was no need for panic or fear of a long exile.

After a short time it appeared that this was, in fact, what had happened. The Arab states had taken their decision to invade Palestine the moment the British mandate came to an end. They wanted the Arab villagers and townspeople out of the way of the fighting. They urged them to seek safety in the neighboring countries while the war lasted, and they promised them it would not last long. As soon as it was over, they would not only come back to their own homes, but they would take over the homes of the Jews, who in the meantime would, in the Arab idiom, have been driven into the sea. Some of the simpler Arabs did not want to go. Their instinct told them to stay where they were, come what might. But most accepted the evacuation order and left, in growing disorder and fright. Those who defied their leaders and remained in their homes are in them to this day. There are scores of Arab villages in Israel, and thousands of Arabs still in the towns; these were people who followed their instinct and not their leaders.

The Arab leaders had been the first to go. Later, in the course of the fighting itself, more Arabs were displaced—there never was a war which did not make refugees. The United Nations at the time estimated the total number of refugees at half a million. Today their number may be nearer nine hundred thousand; it includes some two hundred thousand children born to refugee parents as well as a good many other people registered as refugees despite their coming from places outside Israel. It is a desperate human tragedy—all the more so as there has been no solution in sight. Solutions could have been found if the Arab states had been willing to co-operate in resettling the refugees. This certainly they should have done, since they bear the responsibility for the refugees' having become refugees in the first place. There would have been no refugee problem if the Arab states had not started the war in 1948, and if they had not ordered the people to leave their homes. There has been no acknowledgment on their part of "the debt," to use the words of Dr. Elfan Rees, "which men of the same language, the same faith, the same social organization, should at any time in history feel due from them to their fellows in distress, the debt which in simple terms would involve regarding these people as human beings and not as political footballs." It is a special horror of the refugees' situation that the political opportunism of the Arab states has colored the general approach to their fate. The longer the refugees remain refugees, the more difficult and the more important it becomes not to lose sight of the human tragedy which this bedevilment of their problem involves.

The United Nations began to concern itself with the fate of the refugees at an early stage. In his progress report of September 18, 1948, the UN Mediator had written that the choice was "between saving the lives of many thousands of people now or permitting them to die."* In a supplemental report of October 18 the Acting Mediator declared that the situation of the refugees was critical and that "aid must not only be continued but very greatly increased if disaster is to be averted." Voluntary societies such as the Quakers and the Red Cross had begun relief work, true to their finest traditions, but the problem was becoming too great to be tackled on such a basis alone— particularly as next to no help was being given by the Arab

---

* Count Bernadotte had completed the report shortly before his death on September 17. It was published in New York the day after.

states in which the refugees had gathered. The pattern of Arab policy was beginning to emerge. Without arguing the rights and wrongs of this policy, and indeed without at the time fully comprehending it, the United Nations proceeded to take action. The General Assembly made its first provision for the "relief of Palestine refugees of all communities" on November 19, 1948. Since then at each successive session it has debated the problem and adopted resolutions.

The General Assembly's first decisions on assistance to the refugees were based on the assumption that "the alleviation of conditions of starvation and distress among the Palestine refugees is one of the minimum conditions for the success of the efforts of the United Nations to bring peace to that land." The Secretary-General was authorized to advance immediately a sum up to $5,000,000 for refugee relief. This money was to be drawn from the Working Capital Fund of the United Nations and was to be repaid from the voluntary contributions which all States Members of the United Nations were urged to make toward the $29,500,000 required, on the basis of the Acting Mediator's recommendation, for the period December 1, 1948, to August 31, 1949. At the same time the Assembly requested the Secretary-General "to appoint a Director of United Nations Relief for Palestine Refugees, to whom he may delegate such responsibility as he may consider appropriate for the over-all planning of the relief program."

These measures set the pattern for all future United Nations action on behalf of the Arab refugees. They were extended later in two directions. At its fourth session in the following year, on December 8, 1949, the General Assembly replaced the Director by an Agency called the "United Nations Relief and Works Agency for Palestine Refugees in the Near East" (which came to be known as UNRWAPRNE and later, more simply, as UNRWA). The Agency was

(a) to carry out in collaboration with local governments the direct relief and works programs as recommended by the Economic Survey Mission; *

(b) to consult with the interested Near Eastern Governments concerning measures to be taken by them preparatory to the time when international assistance for relief and works projects is no longer available.

The second extension came with the shift in emphasis from "relief" to "reintegration," foreshadowed by the "works programs" of the Economic Survey Mission. By its fifth session, in the autumn of 1950, the General Assembly had reached the conclusion that "the reintegration of the refugees into the economic life of the Near East, either by repatriation or resettlement, is essential in preparation for the time when international assistance is no longer available, and for the realization of conditions of peace and stability in the area." It instructed UNRWA "to establish a reintegration fund which shall be utilized for projects requested by any Government in the Near East and approved by the Agency for the permanent re-establishment of refugees and their removal from relief." It considered that for the period July 1, 1951, to June 30, 1952, "not less than the equivalent of $30,000,000 should be contributed to the Agency" for this purpose. Just over a year later, at its next session, the Assembly carried this process a long step forward. On January 26, 1952, it endorsed the program recommended by UNRWA, envisaging the expenditure, over

---

* During the summer of 1948 a subsidiary organ of the Palestine Conciliation Commission, known as the Economic Survey Mission for the Middle East, had been established and had visited the area. "This was the first attempt to broaden the approach and to examine the problem against the background of the social realities of the Middle East." *Israel and the United Nations,* National Studies on International Organization (New York, Carnegie Endowment for International Peace, 1956), p. 95.

a three-year period, of $50,000,000 for relief and $200,000,-
000 for reintegration, "over and above such contributions as
may be made by local governments." For the fiscal year beginning July 1, 1952, it approved a budget of $118,000,000, of
which $100,000,000 was to be available for reintegration
and $18,000,000 for relief, and authorized UNRWA to
transfer funds allocated for relief to reintegration (but
not vice versa). It urged "the Governments of the countries
in the area to assist . . . in the carrying out of this program" and asked UNRWA "to explore with the Governments concerned arrangements looking toward their assuming administration of reintegration projects at the earliest
possible date."

The intention of the General Assembly was plain. It did not
wish the refugees to drag out an idle and demoralized existence
on relief; it wanted them to be "reintegrated." "Reintegration" meant resettlement in the Arab countries—as far as
possible, those to which the refugees had gone. Apart altogether from its concern for the refugees, the Assembly had
been finding it increasingly difficult to raise, by voluntary
contributions from governments, the huge sums needed each
year for relief. Governments felt they were pouring money into
a bottomless pit; the sooner the refugees became self-support-
ing, the happier the governments' taxpayers would be. The
brunt of the financial burden was borne by the United States.
The rest was shared by a small number of other contributors,
of whom the highest was Great Britain. Over two thirds of the
members of the United Nations have never contributed a
penny.

If the Assembly's intention was not in doubt, the Arab
states were determined not to heed it. They refused, as they
have refused to this day, to co-operate in projects of reintegration. Instead, they continued to cling to a clause in the
General Assembly's resolution of December 11, 1948 (estab-

lishing the Palestine Conciliation Commission), which they themselves had opposed and voted against:

> that the refugees wishing to return to their homes and live at peace with their neighbors should be permitted to do so at the earliest practicable date, and that compensation should be paid for the property of those choosing not to return and for the loss of or damage to property which, under principles of international law or in equity, should be made good by the Governments or authorities responsible.*

They postulated that all the refugees were entitled to return to their homes and refused to discuss any other aspect of what, even by the time of the Lausanne conference in 1949, had become an extremely complex problem. They were not willing to concede that "the earliest practicable date" could mean anything but "at once," nor that the wish or ability of the refugees to "live at peace with their neighbors" (that is, with the people of Israel) might be affected by the policy adopted toward Israel by the Arab states. The fact that the homes of thousands of refugees had been destroyed in the fighting which the Arab states had started, and that they were no longer there for the refugees to return to, carried no weight. It was to be all or nothing—and very soon it became clear that their true intention was that it should be nothing.

In all this time, the only "Government in the Near East" which co-operated with UNRWA in reintegrating refugees was that of Israel. The end of the war had left some fifty thousand refugees homeless in Israel—people whose homes had been destroyed or who, to escape the fighting where it was

---

* The Palestine Conciliation Commission, after a painstaking survey, estimated the value of immovable property abandoned by the refugees at $280,000,000 and of movable property at another $56,000,000.

thickest, had fled, not across the borders, but to some other part of Israel, and were now D.P.s. The Government of Israel made possible their reintegration by degrees, and UNRWA was able to close its office in Haifa, after "an agreement was concluded with Israel whereby that Government assumed responsibility for the care of the remaining 19,000 refugees in that country as of July 1, 1952."*

Ever since the appointment of the Director of United Nations Relief for Palestine Refugees at the end of 1948, the refugees have had the United Nations to thank for the relatively good conditions in which they live. In the Gaza area, where there are some 60,000 near-destitute Arabs who are not refugees, the contrast between them and the refugees maintained by the United Nations is particularly striking—in housing, nutrition, and health and educational facilities. UNRWA, with the help of the specialized agencies of the United Nations and some voluntary societies, has not only kept the refugees alive and well, but has provided schooling for the children and vocational training for the young. It could not, of course, have done anything but for the generosity of the governments which have contributed the funds. Everything that international aid could do to relieve this great human tragedy has been done, and if UNRWA's plans for reintegrating the refugees in productive occupations have come to nothing, it is not primarily the fault of the United Nations. At the same time, the reintegration problem has never been faced squarely, as

---

* Annual Report of the Director of UNRWA, July 1, 1951, to June 30, 1952, UN General Assembly, Official Records, Seventh Session, Supplement No. 13 (A/2171), p. 3. In May 1949 there were 142,000 Arabs in Israel, including 25,000 in the districts incorporated under the armistice agreement with Jordan. By mid-1957 their number had risen to over 200,000 by natural increase and the return of former residents (refugees).

a result of the United Nations' inability to overcome the political opposition of the Arab states.

The international community tried to see to it that the refugees were kept alive until the day they could cease to be refugees. The Arab states have seen to it that the refugee problem has been kept alive, and that that day should never dawn. There have been many refugee situations in the post-war world grimmer than that of the Arab refugees.* They have not been kept so constantly before world opinion, because no one had a political interest in keeping them there. When fifteen million Moslems and Hindus were displaced as a result of the partition of India, the Governments of India and Pakistan set about their relief and reintegration as a matter of course. Relatively little was heard about their plight, because India and Pakistan each accepted the task of solving the problem, regarding this as their natural duty. Repatriation was never thought of, since clearly the Moslems could be assimilated more easily in Pakistan, to which they had fled, and the Hindus similarly in India. The United Nations was able to undertake relief and rehabilitation of the refugees in Korea without undue fuss or trouble, operating through its agencies, UNKRA and UNCURK, which were parallel to UNRWA in every way except one—they did not have artificial political complications to contend with. No one suggested that the two and a half million who fled from North to South Korea should be repatriated. On any sensible and human view, the problem of the Arab refugees could long ago have

---

* It has been estimated that in Asia alone, excluding the Middle East, over twenty-six million people have been uprooted and become refugees since the end of the Second World War. The total for the whole world is fifty-seven million. These figures were quoted at the Geneva conference on The Refugee Problem—To-day and To-morrow, May 27–28, 1957.

been settled by their reintegration in the Arab states—particularly as Israel had in the meantime herself resettled in her territory nearly half a million Jewish refugees from the Arab countries.

But the Arab states were quick to see that they had in the refugees a priceless political asset. They were determined to do everything to preserve it—which meant doing nothing for the refugees. The refugee problem will not be solved unless an Arab state, say Iraq, acquires a practical interest in the absorption of refugees, strong enough to outweigh considerations of general Arab policy, or until this policy itself is changed. The Arab states as a whole will have no interest in the solution of the problem until the refugees become a political liability for them, as they have been for Israel, or at least cease to be an asset. This, in turn, depends on the attitude of the rest of the world, which so far has been content to provide relief for the refugees and to surrender to the Arab states' insistence that it should provide relief alone.

The Smith-Prouty report* was almost the first to analyze the situation correctly. Its authors, approaching it from the point of view of their own country, which provided the bulk of the relief funds, recommended that "the United States should serve notice that it will not support the return of the Arab refugees to their former homes within the boundaries of Israel under existing conditions." (They recognized that repatriation was impossible, and inferentially that the Arab states were demanding it only because they knew it to be impossible. Even if it were technically possible, which it never was, it would be laying up far greater dangers for the future than the integration of the Arab refugees among their own kith and kin.) The United States, the report urged, should announce that it would contribute no further assistance to the

---

* Pp. 6, 9. *Cf.* p. 119.

refugees, as such, after a specified future date. This "would put the refugees and the Arab governments on notice that the status quo cannot be maintained indefinitely." Further, the United States "should indicate its willingness to contribute to the development of countries which provide homes for refugees and admit them to equal rights with their own citizens." At the same time, the United States, it was recommended, "should press for compensation by Israel to refugees for real and personal property lost."

As is the fate of parliamentary papers, the Smith-Prouty report, published on February 25, 1954, was shelved and forgotten. But it has lost none of its validity. The two Congressmen, in an on-the-spot investigation in the autumn of 1953, had seen the situation clearly. The whole world sympathizes with refugees. It sympathized at once with the Arab refugees, just as a few years earlier it had sympathized spontaneously with the Jewish refugees from Nazi persecution. It is prepared, too, to extend its sympathy to those who speak in the name of the refugees. The Zionist movement drew some of its postwar strength from the world's readiness to help the Jewish D.P.s in the concentration camps, for whose future it was able to formulate a constructive solution—the establishment of a Jewish state. This kind of sympathy becomes a powerful political weapon. The Arab states, representing themselves as spokesmen for the Arab refugees, were quick to divert to their own political ends the sympathy which the world gave to the refugees—but which it had no reason to give to the Arab states for their own sakes. It did not occur to anyone to scrutinize their credentials or inquire into their motives. The Arab national cause as a whole became the beneficiary of the sympathy which was intended for the refugees alone. This was a political achievement which had to be consolidated at any price. The price had to be paid by the refugees, who were now destined to remain refugees in the political interest of the

Arab states. The Arab states were able to maintain this happy situation as long as they could conceal from the rest of the world that it was *they* who blocked a solution of the refugee problem. They could do this best by making the world believe that it was Israel which was responsible for the refugees' becoming refugees in the first place and remaining refugees ever since. They proceeded to do this by a propaganda campaign which the world, not at once recognizing its falseness, for long allowed to succeed. There has, indeed, been no excuse since Lausanne for not perceiving the object of the Arab campaign, but it is only in the last two or three years that world opinion has awakened to it fully.

Congressmen Smith and Prouty were the forerunners of this awakening. They understood that as long as the refugees remained a major political asset for the Arab states, there was no hope of solving the refugee problem. It could be turned into a political liability for these states in one way only—by opening the eyes of the world to the fact that the Arab states could solve the problem but refused to. The world's sympathy would turn to scorn, and the Arab states would have every inducement to rid themselves of the refugee problem quickly. By stipulating that there would be no further payments for relief unless the Arab states agreed to co-operate in the resettlement of the refugees, the United Nations would be putting the responsibility for the fate of the refugees squarely on these states—which is where it belongs. If they refused to co-operate, the whole world would see at once who, and who alone, was to blame for the continued homelessness and demoralization of the refugees. The Arab states, to escape the liability, would find themselves constrained to reverse their policy.

This would be, in theory, quite feasible even now. The funds were voted by the General Assembly six years ago and would still be available. UNRWA has worked out detailed plans for resettlement, calculating that the entire process can be completed between a minimum of three and a maximum of five years. Contributing governments would be glad to continue paying for relief if they knew this was a diminishing liability which would liquidate itself in five years at the most, instead of being, as it is now, a drain on their resources whose end no one can foresee. Above all, the refugees themselves, after nine years of aimlessness and despair, would again stand on their own feet, productive workers in a community to which by every criterion of race, religion and language they belong.

There would be nothing to prevent achievement of this program, if the world were prepared to risk the fury of the Arab states. This is not as easy now as it would have been even a few years ago, before the cold war spread to the Middle East.

But it is not impossible. Israel, for her part, would make her own maximum contribution toward the final settlement, and would make it gladly. She accepted the principle of compensation as long ago as 1949 and stands by it still. In practice, as Mr. Eban pointed out in the General Assembly in 1955, "payment of compensation would require the solution and clarification of related problems. . . . The Arab governments cannot attempt to stifle Israel financially by blockade and boycott, and at the same time expect Israel to assume heavy financial burdens for this and future generations of its citizens. The Arab governments will one day have to decide whether the pleasures of an illicit blockade are more to be cherished than the affirmative duty of enabling the refugees to receive compensation." But the Arabs' boycott and blockade, like their political exploitation of the refugees, could not have attained the dimensions they have, had it not been for the inertness of the rest of the world. The problems are interlocked—and not beyond the wit of man to resolve.

The refugees were a gift to Arab propaganda, which succeeded, by perverting the facts, in turning them into the gravest political liability with which Israel has had to contend in the first decade of her existence. Wherever in the "Western" world anti-Israel feeling exists, it draws its inspiration primarily from the Arab refugees. For all her efforts, Israel has never succeeded in freeing herself from the reproach leveled at her by Arab propaganda—that she drove out the refugees in the first place and has since cruelly denied them the elementary human right of "returning home," and that in doing so she has "defied" the United Nations. The world accepted the specious claim of the Arab states that they were concerned for the good of the Arab refugees. Despite her constant recital of the facts, Israel failed to demolish this assumption of Arab good faith, and from it flowed, inevitably, political conclusions which were bound to harm her. But the Arabs, in time, overreached themselves. Today the truth about the refugees, expressed neatly by the Iraqi Minister, is no longer concealed.

The question naturally arises whether, now that the truth is out, it is likely to be made a basis for action. This must depend largely on the readiness and capacity of the United States. In the spring of 1957, Senator Hubert H. Humphrey, a member of the U. S. Senate's Committee on Foreign Relations, visited the Middle East and on his return home submitted a report * in which he propounded four assumptions as "the only realistic basis for an effective American policy toward the Middle East":

1. That Israel is an integral part of the region and is there to stay;

2. That the 1949 armistice boundaries constitute inviolable political boundaries subject to change only by the joint agreement of the states concerned;

---

* *The Middle East and Southern Europe,* Report of Senator Hubert H. Humphrey on a study mission (Washington, United States Government Printing Office, 1957).

THE FIRST TEN YEARS

3. That resettlement in Arab lands, with compensation for property left in Israel, is in fact the only effective and realistic way of solving the Arab refugee problem;

4. That the stability and security of the region demand an early settlement of the Arab-Israeli conflict.

Senator Humphrey devoted special attention to the refugee problem, which he presents as "a challenge to the conscience of humanity." He believes, particularly of the younger generation of refugees, that "to return them now to an alien society they have been taught to despise would be as self-defeating and unsatisfactory as abandoning them to mature in the appalling atmosphere of hopelessness which now pervades the refugee camps. The destiny of these young Arabs clearly lies in an opportunity for a productive and self-reliant life in an Arab environment and culture." Repatriation is in any case no longer possible. Israel, the Senator recalls, "has accepted and settled some 900,000 immigrants, many of whom were in fact refugees from Arab States where repressive measures have made their lives intolerable. Furthermore, surrounded by nations which insist upon exercising rights of belligerency against her, it would be suicidal for Israel to admit a large group of immigrants whose whole indoctrination for the past 10 years has been one of hatred for the Jewish state. To do so would be to establish a fifth column inside the country." From the viewpoint of the refugees themselves, repatriation to Israel would result in bitter disillusionment: "they would necessarily have to live in a society foreign to their own background and culture, and assume all the obligations of citizenship in a state which they have been taught to despise."

Senator Humphrey concludes that "the facts of the situation themselves point to the only possible solution—the provision for the vast majority of permanent homes and tolerable livelihoods in the Arab States, and a commitment by Israel to accept a limited number of token repatriates." He recommends that "all of these things" should be carefully explored by a new United Nations Good Offices Commission, whose duty it would be "to press resolutely and unremittingly for a breakthrough on this critical refugee problem."

Whatever the merits of this or that point in Senator Humphrey's recommendations, he is probably right in believing that the problem should be dealt with through the United Nations, if it cannot be solved on their own by the countries immediately concerned. Direct action by the United States might well achieve the opposite of the effect desired, now that the Arab states are wrestling with the forces of cold war. But United Nations action will not be taken except on United States initiative, and it will not be effective unless the problem is tackled in the first place in terms of politics. There will be no point in assuming, as the General Assembly did for years, that reintegration must be feasible *eo ipso*—being right and good in itself, and clearly to the benefit of the refugees. The Arab states have for too long used the refugees as "political hostages in their struggle with Israel," to quote one of Senator Humphrey's phrases. They have fought reintegration, to take another, "lest political leverage over Israel be lost." No action to aid the refugees can hope to succeed if it is not based on recognition of this central fact.

7

Power Pressures in the Middle East

THE DIPLOMATIC REPRESENTATIVES of the United States and the Soviet Union were the first to come to Israel. They arrived within a few days of one another, early in August 1948. In a Tel Aviv packed to the rafters, they found lodging under the same modest roof. The hotel put up two flagstaffs, from which Stars and Stripes and Hammer and Sickle fluttered side by side. Even at that time this was a sufficiently unusual sight to attract press photographers, and for weeks newspapers in every part of the world featured the upper stories of the Gat Rimmon Hotel. The people of Israel saw it as an omen. Israel, beset by Arab armies, could lean on the support of the two mightiest nations on earth. More than this—there was a feeling that Israel had somehow brought East and West together. If they could act in concert, or at least in step, on Israel, why should they not come to agree on other things? The messianism latent in the Jewish soul, stimulated by the miracle of Israel's rebirth, was ready to embrace the entire world. With the fulfillment of Biblical prophecy, a new era of peace and good will could be dawning for all men.*

Israel longed desperately to be on good terms with all nations, but especially, and equally, with the United States and the Soviet Union. The feat did not seem impossible. On March 9, 1949, the Knesset approved, among the "basic principles" of the new Government's program, "loyalty to the principles of the United Nations Charter and friendship with all freedom-loving States, and in particular with the United States and the Soviet Union." Three months earlier Mr. Ben Gurion had told America's Special Representative in Israel: "I will never play politics with an issue of foreign policy." † Other party leaders followed his example, and the country has never deviated, in principle, from its ideal of friendship with all the world. In practice, it discovered soon enough that it is one thing to want to be friends and quite another to achieve friendship. Its policy of "nonidentification" could not survive the crisis of Korea. Mr. Sharett, speaking in the Knesset immediately after the outbreak of war there, showed himself aware of this:

---

* Mr. Ben Gurion, in a statement issued the day after the General Assembly's resolution of November 29, 1947, had expressed the same idea more guardedly: "The co-operation of America and Russia in a solution of the Palestine problem is bound to serve as an encouragement to all those who, in common with the Jewish people, believe in the possibility of permanent co-operation between East and West for the furtherance of permanent peace in the world."

† James G. McDonald, *My Mission in Israel* (New York, Simon and Schuster, Inc., 1951), p. 104.

The principle of nonidentification is Israel's way of serving world peace, of making specific her contribution toward preventing a widening of the breach and perhaps, within her restricted means, of helping to narrow and heal the breach. But this principle . . . cannot be perverted into a repudiation of world peace, nor can it serve as a pretext for running away from responsibility toward the United Nations, nor can it be turned into a weapon which instead of preserving peace might well affect the security of Israel herself.

Only a few weeks before, on May 25, 1950, the United States, Great Britain and France, after a meeting of their Foreign Ministers in London, had issued a declaration regarding armaments and security in the Middle East. The three Governments had stated that they "recognize that the Arab States and Israel all need to maintain a certain level of armed forces for the purpose of assuring their internal security and their legitimate self-defense and *to permit them to play their part in the defense of the area as a whole*." (The italics were not in the original.) All applications for arms or war material for these countries would be considered in the light of these principles, the three Powers at the same time reiterating "their opposition to the development of an arms race between the Arab States and Israel." The declaration concluded:

> The three Governments take this opportunity of declaring their deep interest in and their desire to promote the establishment and the maintenance of peace and stability in the area and their unalterable opposition to the use of force or threat of force between any of the States in that area. The three Governments, should they find that any of these States was preparing to violate frontiers or armistice lines, would, consistently with their obligations as members of the United

Nations, immediately take action, both within and outside the United Nations, to prevent such violation.

The Three-Power Declaration, as it came to be known, was issued without previous consultation either with Israel or with the Arab states. It was simply communicated to them for their information. Israel regarded it as a unilateral declaration which was not binding on her, though she welcomed it, as Mr. Ben Gurion told the Knesset a few days later, "to the extent that it was designed to increase security and peace." The Government of Israel hoped that the three Powers would now stop discriminating against Israel in the supply of arms and "received with particular satisfaction the wish of the three Powers to promote peace and stability in the Middle East, and their objection to the use of force by any State in this part of the world."

"Defense of the area as a whole," in the language of the Western Powers, meant defense against Soviet attack. The Soviet Union, for its part, has always seen Western plans for defense of the Middle East as the beginning of aggression against itself. The global struggle between East and West was now superimposed on the local tug-of-war between the Arab states and Israel, and the two were never again to be disentangled. As far as the Arab states were concerned, they were now started along the road which was to lead Egypt and Syria close to the Soviet Union, and Iraq into foundation membership in the Baghdad Pact. The fight for the soul of Jordan, which was to come to a head in 1957, was, in proportions not easy to determine, partly a struggle for power between rival Arab factions and partly a trial of strength between the Soviet Union and the United States. In this extraordinarily complex situation, the position of Israel could never be easy. The Arab states, divided by conflicting ambitions, were united only in their hostility toward Israel. The United States and the Soviet

Union, maneuvering for position in the Middle East, outbid one another for the favors of the Arab states. Israel, so anxious to love and be loved, found herself elbowed aside. Her main thought, inevitably, was for her own security, menaced by the Arab states; and it was this consideration, above all others, which guided her Government at each stage of a rapidly deteriorating situation.

On October 13, 1951, a few weeks after Turkey's admission to membership in NATO, the Western Powers informed Israel of their decision to establish an Allied Middle East Command, "in which countries able and willing to contribute to the defense of the area should participate." They conveyed the opinion of NATO that the defense of the Middle East, which was vital to the security of the "free world," could be secured only through the co-operation of the interested Powers, including those not territorially part of the area. In view of "the paramount importance to the Command of bases in Egypt," the Egyptian Government was being invited to participate as a founder member "on a basis of equality and partnership with the other founder members."

The delicacy and ambivalence of Israel's position were immediately apparent. On the one hand, Israel could not afford to be left out of a scheme which must vastly increase Egypt's military strength. She believed that Egypt would never, in practice, use this strength for the "defense of the area as a whole," but only, as soon as there was enough of it, against herself. With Egypt's record in the Second World War fresh in the public mind, Israel thought the Western Powers naïve for believing that Egypt would side with them against the Soviet Union. If there was going to be an armed clash between East and West, Egypt would sit on the fence until the last minute and then, as in 1945, join the side which to all intents and purposes had won. But if Israel could not afford to be left out of a scheme which, as she saw it, was going to strengthen Egypt at her expense, she was not eager, on the other hand, to be dragged into political conflict with the Soviet Union. Even if she joined only a defense organization, the Soviet Union would see her as one of the Powers conspiring for aggression.

As it happened, the scheme for a Middle East Command, as originally conceived, quickly fell through, as a result of Egypt's refusal to join it. But the three Powers and Turkey, now appearing as "the four associated Governments," at once informed the Arab states that although they regretted Egypt's decision, their own determination to establish the Middle East Command could not be "deflected or delayed." They were not, "at the present time," inviting the Arab states to associate themselves with the Command, but they hoped that these states would "seriously consider what the Middle East Command means in terms of their welfare and security." As for Israel, her views would be welcomed later, "when the sponsoring Powers have proceeded further in the organization" of the Command. The Turkish Minister to Israel, presenting an *aide-mémoire,* made the meaning of this plain when he said that in his Government's view the "tense relations" prevailing between the Arab states and Israel were a "retarding factor" in the plans for Middle Eastern defense. Turkey hoped that Israel would adopt a "realistic attitude"—in other words, Israel should stand aside, at least until all the Arab states were safely in the net. The three Powers, when they had informed Israel two weeks earlier of their invitation to Egypt, had expressed themselves as "well aware of the difficulties which will arise over the association of Israel and the Arab states with one and the same Command organization." They would do everything in their power to resolve these difficulties, but Israel was left under no illusions. The Middle East Command would be organized without her—and the Arab states would be supplied with arms, while she would not. Sixteen months of war in Korea had changed the face of the world. The three Powers had traveled a long way since declaring their "opposition to the development of an arms race" the year before.*

The following years saw Israel constantly straining to draw level with the Arab states, or as nearly level as she could, in terms of armament and military equipment, and the Arab states determined to preserve and if possible increase their lead. Arab Governments called on their people to prepare for the "second round," meanwhile laying in arms from Great Britain and the United States, while Israel knocked vainly at London and Washington doors. Israel felt that Great Britain and the United States, which were supplying Arab states with arms for defense, could not, if they remained true to their own policy, deny her arms for the same purpose. She heard herself bombarded daily by Arab threats and had every reason to fear that the neighboring states, accepting Western arms ostensibly for defense, would in fact use them to attack her as soon as they had enough. When in the autumn of 1955 Egypt signed a contract with Czechoslovakia for the supply, on an unprecedented scale, of modern arms, including aircraft and tanks, Israel was convinced that the "second round" could not be delayed much longer.

In the late evening of February 9, 1953, shortly before the death of Stalin, a small bomb exploded in the garden of the

---

* The three Powers themselves denied that there was any change in their policy regarding an arms race. On November 9, 1951, they stated that the Middle East Command would dedicate itself to "the defense of the area as a whole against outside aggression." It would "not interfere in problems and disputes arising within the area." It in no way affected "existing arrangements relating to such matters," including the Tripartite Declaration of May 1950. In practice, from now on, each of the Arab states, with the possible exception of Yemen, received arms from one or more of the three Powers, in fulfillment of existing treaty obligations, of new treaty obligations undertaken in the course of these years, and of ordinary commercial contracts.

Soviet Legation at Tel Aviv. At this time the "doctors' plot" had been fabricated in Moscow (according to later Soviet explanations, by Beria), and a campaign was on foot against "Zionists" and "cosmopolitans." The Soviet Government at once held the Israel Government responsible for the outrage and broke off diplomatic relations. They were renewed in July of the same year, after an exchange of correspondence in which Israel gave assurances that she would not join any aggressive alliance against the Soviet Union. These assurances had been sought by the Soviet Government, whose definition of "aggression" was not necessarily the same as that of Israel. The new American Secretary of State, Mr. John Foster Dulles, had visited the Middle East, including Israel, in May. On his return to Washington, he had delivered an address to the American people, on June 1, 1953, and touched on the question of Middle East defense:

A Middle East Defense Organization is a future rather than an immediate possibility. Many of the Arab League countries are so engrossed with their quarrels with Israel or with Great Britain or France that they pay little heed to the menace of Soviet Communism. However, there is more concern where the Soviet Union is near. In general, the northern tier of nations shows awareness of the danger. There is a vague desire to have a collective security system. But no such system can be imposed from without. It should be designed and grow from within out of a sense of common destiny and common danger.

Here was the seed of the Baghdad Pact organization, which was to flower from the treaty concluded between Turkey and Iraq on February 24, 1955. The Soviet Union was determined that Israel, at least, should not join any such system. It need have had no fear. The Turco-Iraqi treaty, while inviting other countries to adhere to it, was accompanied by an exchange of letters which restricted adherence to countries recognized by the signatories. This device, introduced at Iraq's insistence, was designed to avert any danger of Israel's wanting to join. Iraq had, of course, not recognized her. Israel experienced again the conflicting emotions she knew so well—frustration at her forced exclusion from an enterprise in which she alone of all the Middle Eastern states could never be a partner, relief at not having to choose whether to adhere to the Baghdad Pact or not. If Israel had been free to decide whether or not to join a Middle East defense scheme, she might well have decided to join. But she would have done so less from faith in the effectiveness or desirability of such schemes than from a wish not to be left out in the cold, watching the Arabs receive arms which she was denied.

"Arms for Israel" became the refrain, *crescendo*, of speakers in the Knesset, of Israel's representatives abroad, and of friends everywhere who understood the rising threat to Israel's security. With Great Britain there was not a chance. The British Government held that in assessing the military strength of Israel relative to that of the Arab states, account had to be taken of elements other than arms—Israel's leadership and morale, for example, and the quality of her manpower. Israel argued in vain that the highest morale and the bravest men could not prevail against the vastly superior weapons of the other side. The United States, too, refused to accede to Israel's requests—until, by the beginning of 1956, the case had become overwhelming. It then intimated to the Governments of Canada and France that, while it could itself not sell arms to Israel, it would have no objection to their doing so. The Canadian Government, which had a sound appreciation of Middle Eastern affairs, was immediately helpful. The French had not waited for an American *placet* to reach Paris. Months earlier, they had sensed the grave danger in which Israel stood as the result of Egypt's arms deal with Czechoslovakia. Striving all the time to persuade the United States of Israel's urgent need, they had begun to help her generously on their own account.

France had shown a deep understanding for the Jewish people's needs even before Israel achieved independence. She had rendered the Jewish cause decisive material and moral aid in times of great stress. The amity between the two countries established in those early years was now to rise to a point at which it transcended anything Israel had ever known. The popularity of France among all sections of the people was reflected undiminished in the graver counsels of state. France and Israel were friends.

With the intensification of the East-West struggle in the Middle East, Israel found herself increasingly isolated. The more she sought escape from this isolation, the crueler her dilemma became. Inaction was impossible as she saw the Arabs courted by both sides and gaining daily in political and military strength. The instinct of self-preservation alone would have spurred her Government to action.

As ever greater exertions were made to ensure Israel's security, her weakness was more dangerously exposed. On the Soviet side the die had been cast. The Soviet Government believed that through hostility to Israel lay the highroad to Arab hearts. With characteristic realism it took that road and would not be deflected from it. The Moscow doctors who were accused of killing Soviet leaders and plotting to kill others were, according to a Tass announcement of January 13, 1953, "closely connected with the Jewish international nationalistic bourgeois organization . . . set up by American intelligence for so-called material assistance to Jews in other countries." *Pravda,* on the same day, spoke of "the hideous face of this Zionist espionage organization." There was no specific mention of Israel; the doctors were accused of being hirelings of the American and British intelligence services. But the reference to Zionism was ominous. Against the background of the Slansky trial which had ended seven weeks earlier in Prague, it justified the liveliest alarm. A communication received on February 5, 1953, from the Czechoslovak Government did nothing to dissipate Israel's apprehensions. Lashing out at "the effrontery and arrogance of the Israel Zionist agents in Czechoslovakia" and "the American warmongers and their Israeli and other stooges," it alleged that "the ruling circles of Israel and the Zionist organizations which they lead and represent . . . are under the orders of the financially most powerful Zionist groups in the United States and . . . consciously supply a willing instrument for the warmongering policy of American imperialism."

This was balm to the Arabs—and not calculated to make the United States seek closer association with Israel. Israel, for her part, increasingly anxious for her security as blow after blow rained in from the East, had no choice but to seek salvation in the West. She began to think in terms of a security guarantee, to be given, if possible, by all or most of the Powers which had interests in the Middle East, or, if this proved impossible, by the United States alone. But all Israel's efforts to obtain such a guarantee, or to conclude a bilateral security pact with the United States, failed, as they were bound to, on account of the inherent weakness of her position. Precisely because she was under attack from the other major forces in the Middle East, the Arabs and the Soviet Union, Israel could not attract the Western Powers. There was never any prospect, as the Soviet Government must in its heart of hearts have known, of Israel's becoming an instrument of American "warmongering." The United States, like the Soviet Union, sought its allies in the Moslem and Arab world, where in due course it found them—in Turkey, Iraq, Iran, Pakistan and Saudi Arabia.

The Arab states, in the meantime, had been hurrying forward their military planning against Israel. The "Joint Defense and Economic Co-operation Treaty," concluded by all the Arab states on June 17, 1950, furnished the basis. It set up a Permanent Military Commission and a Joint Defense Council, whose functions were transparent. In addition, a series of pacts was concluded between two or more Arab states,* culminating in the establishment, on October 24, 1956, of a unified military command by Egypt, Jordan and Syria. No effort was made by these countries to conceal their purpose. *Al Gomhouria*, the official organ of the Egyptian military junta, on October 27 stated that the unified command had been set up "in a supreme effort to tighten the death noose" around Israel. On the same date, Abdullah Rimawi, who was three days later to become Foreign Minister of Jordan, varied the metaphor only slightly when he spoke of the command as "completing the ring of steel round Israel's neck." On October 28 Taufiq Nizam ed-Din, the Syrian Chief of Staff, declared that the agreement had been concluded "to unify Arab military action against the common enemy." Israel had no fancy to be garrotted. The following night saw the launching of the Sinai campaign as an urgent act of self-defense. Mobilization had begun four days earlier, immediately after the establishment of the unified command.

The campaign, which in five days cleared the Egyptian army out of Gaza and the Sinai desert, transformed Israel's position

---

* The most important were the revised Joint Defense Treaty concluded by Egypt, Iraq, Syria, Lebanon and Saudi Arabia in 1951, to which Jordan adhered in 1952 and Yemen in 1953; the Joint Defense Agreements between Egypt and Syria and Egypt and Saudi Arabia respectively, both in 1955; the Joint Defense Agreement signed by Egypt, Saudi Arabia and Yemen in 1956; and the declarations on military co-ordination and co-operation made by Jordan and Syria on the one hand and by Egypt and Jordan on the other, also in 1956.

in the area. Apart altogether from its military lessons, which were not lost on the United States and the Soviet Union any more than they were on the Arabs, it freed Israel from the menace of attack by the neighboring states, at least for the immediate future. A damper was put on talk of the "second round." In fulfillment of their treaty obligations, all the other Arab states should have come at once to the help of Egypt, but none of them did. Saudi Arabia, Syria and Iraq took the opportunity of sending forces into Jordan, but they advanced no farther. Arab self-respect should have crumpled altogether under this blow which the Arabs themselves dealt it. The fact that it did not, and that the Arab states (including Egypt) were quick with their excuses, suggested to some that they had never intended their treaty obligations to be taken quite as seriously as the written word and their public statements implied. There was a political lesson here too for the Powers: without the backing of overwhelming force there could be no relying on Arab states to respect their obligations.

The United States and the Soviet Union, each in its way, bore down heavily on Israel—but the Arab states did not come out of the encounter with honor. The United States cut off all economic aid to Israel and came within inches of supporting a movement for "sanctions" against her in the UN General Assembly. The Soviet Union, accusing Israel of "acting as an instrument of external imperialistic forces," and of "criminally and irresponsibly playing with the fate of the world," withdrew its ambassador from Israel* (without, however, breaking off diplomatic relations as it had done in 1953). It stopped all shipments of oil to Israel, in violation of contracts binding until 1958. Marshal Bulganin, chairman of the U.S.S.R. Council of Ministers, sent two strongly worded letters to Mr. Ben

---

* The ambassador returned five months later, on April 6, 1957. American aid to Israel was resumed at about the same time.

Gurion. President Eisenhower and Mr. Dulles, in less hector-
ing terms, made their disapproval as clear. By this time the
rivalry between East and West for decisive influence in the
Middle East had become so acute that there was genuine fear
of a third world war. Israel was told that she would bear the
responsibility for such a disaster. The tension, rising to near-
hysteria at the United Nations, where the General Assembly
had been called into emergency session, was at once relieved
by Israel's decision to withdraw her forces from Egypt.* Far
from wishing to start a third world war, Israel had wanted only
to avert the general Middle Eastern war which had been
brought to the brink of realization by the build-up of powerful
Egyptian military forces on her borders and the establishment
of the unified military command by Egypt, Syria and Jordan.

If there was widespread fear of world war in the wake of
the Sinai campaign, it did not, of course, spring primarily from
the campaign as such. It arose in particular from the military
intervention of Great Britain and France. Israel herself, provoked beyond endurance by Arab threats and incessant guerrilla raiding, had struck back against Egypt by a swift military
blow which she saw, in all truth, as a necessity of self-defense.
If this had been all, the two countries could have been left to
fight it out among themselves. But Great Powers, like nature,
abhor a vacuum. The Middle East was no longer an area whose
inhabitants were free to settle their own relations as best they
could. Everything now had to be seen and done in the light of

---

* In a communication to the Secretary-General of the United Nations
on November 8, 1956, the Foreign Minister of Israel informed him that
"the Government of Israel will willingly withdraw its forces from
Egypt immediately upon the conclusion of satisfactory arrangements
with the United Nations in connection with the emergency international force." At the same time the United Nations was asked "to call
upon Egypt . . . to enter into direct peace negotiations with Israel."

the struggle between East and West. There had been few illusions about this, at least since the Tripartite Declaration and the war in Korea. Lingering doubts or hopes were dissipated by the exertions of the West to organize Middle Eastern defense and the parallel efforts of the East to establish a foothold in Egypt and Syria. World reactions to the Sinai campaign made it clear that by the end of 1956 no further illusions existed anywhere. For five years, from 1945 to 1950, the main theater of the cold war was in Europe. For the next five years, from the outbreak of hostilities in Korea till after the end of the fighting in Indo-China, it shifted to the Far East. By 1955, after preliminary skirmishes in the area, the cold war centered squarely on the Middle East. It will remain there, one must assume, until—perhaps by 1960—a *modus vivendi* or stalemate is reached on the European and Far Eastern patterns.

For the peoples of the area this is a thoroughly uncomfortable situation. Their own relationships are not eased by it. All the Great Powers have at various times in the past ten years expressed a desire—at least platonically—for peace between the Arab states and Israel. But their policies have, in practice, not worked for such a peace. In the opinion of many, they have, if anything, worked against it. Israel-Arab peace, however desirable in itself, has never been an overriding interest of any of the Powers. They have never pursued it single-mindedly with all the means at their disposal, as they have pursued other objectives, in the Middle East and elsewhere. The conflict between the Arab states and Israel, far from undermining the position of any of the Great Powers, has not been without its uses. This situation has naturally operated in favor of the Arabs. Not wanting peace in the first place, they have been encouraged, by the indifference or inactivity of the Powers, to persist in refusing it. Peace has seemed to them to offer fewer prizes than the absence of it.

From time to time ideas have been thrown out for the

neutralization of the Middle East. In its original form, the plan was confined to a general arms embargo for the area. Israel was ready to accept this, on the understanding that the Arab states would really receive no arms. Since she herself needed arms only for defense against Arab attack, she would have been ready to do without them if no such danger existed. But the notion of an arms embargo was inconsistent with the situation as it had developed since 1955. With the Soviet Union shipping arms in abundance to Egypt and Syria, the two self-styled "neutralists," it appeared to many that neutralization of the Middle East would be but a euphemism for Soviet control. On April 17, 1956, the Soviet Government had issued an important policy statement, attributing the "aggravation of the international situation in the Middle and Near East" to "the continued attempts to form and encourage military groupings serving the ends of colonialism and directed against the independence of the peoples of this region as well as against the security of peace-loving countries." The statement went on:

> The principles of respecting national independence and sovereignty, and of nonintervention in the internal affairs of states, as well as the settlement of international disputes by peaceful means, are enshrined in the Charter of the United Nations. In its consistent adherence to these principles, the Soviet Government has lent and is lending sincere and wholehearted support to the aspirations of the Arab states, to a further strengthening of their recently gained national independence and to the enhancement of their economic welfare. . . . In so doing, the Soviet Government has sought no special advantages for itself but aimed at regularizing its relations with the states of this region on the basis of the just principles proclaimed by the peoples of Asia and Africa at the Bandung Conference.

Despite a reference earlier in the statement to the sympathy and support which the Soviet Union had extended to the "establishment and strengthening of the political independence of Egypt, Saudi Arabia, Syria, Lebanon, Yemen, Jordan, Libya, Sudan, Iraq, Israel, etc.," Israel, which had been excluded from Bandung,* found small comfort in this emphasis on the aspirations of the Arab states. But the declaration with which the statement ended aroused hopes:

> The Soviet Union holds that in order to strengthen international peace and security it is imperative to direct efforts toward a peaceful and durable settlement of the Palestine question on a mutually acceptable basis, bearing in mind the legitimate national interests of the parties concerned.

This seemed to come near to Israel's wish for negotiations with the Arab states, with a view to settling the conflict "on a mutually acceptable basis"—that is, by agreement. The Arabs understood the Soviet declaration in the same sense and immediately criticized it on this account. Little more was subsequently heard of this aspect of Soviet policy, apart from an allusion to it in the note sent to the Western Powers on February 11 of the following year. By the spring of 1956 the Soviet Union had built up such a position of ascendancy in Egypt that it might easily have pressed its point further. But no sooner did it encounter opposition to the reasonable idea of a settlement "on a mutually acceptable basis" than it stopped short in its tracks, like other Powers before it. Since the resumption of diplomatic relations in 1953, this was the first titbit Israel had received at the Soviet table, only to see it vanish before it could be properly savored.

Early in 1957 the Eisenhower Doctrine opened a new phase in America's unfolding plans for the defense of the Middle

---

* *Cf.* pp. 184-188.

East. There was no indication now, as there had been at the time of the Allied Middle East Command in 1951, that the inclusion of Israel was not desired. For the first time, Israel was to be directly involved. The Doctrine, as approved by the Congress of the United States on March 9, 1957, defined four principles which were to govern American policy in the Middle East. The President was authorized to co-operate with and assist nations of the area in "the development of economic strength dedicated to the maintenance of national independence." Israel, which had been receiving American economic aid on a generous scale almost from the moment of her birth and was determined at all costs to maintain her national independence, had no difficulty in accepting this principle. The President was authorized, further, to "undertake military assistance programs" with any nation or group of nations in the area desiring such assistance. This was what Israel had been asking, for herself, for years. The third principle was unexceptionable (and bore a remarkable likeness, *mutatis mutandis,* to principles laid down in the Soviet Government's statement of the year before): "The United States regards as vital to the national interest and world peace the preservation of the independence and integrity of the nations of the Middle East." It was the fourth principle which aroused such controversy in Israel that for a time the stability of the Government coalition was shaken:

> To this end, if the President determines the necessity thereof, the United States is prepared to use armed forces to assist any such nation or group of such nations requesting assistance against armed aggression from any country controlled by international communism: *Provided,* That such employment shall be consonant with the treaty obligations of the United States and with the Constitution of the United States.

The United States made an exceptional effort to secure the endorsement of these principles by the countries of the Middle East. In the course of a tour of the area, which for purposes of the Doctrine extended from Morocco to Pakistan, Ambassador James P. Richards visited Israel and conferred with the Government. The only countries omitted from his tour were Egypt and Syria, both under Soviet influence, and Jordan, where the visit of President Eisenhower's special envoy would have embarrassed King Hussein at the climax of his campaign to wrest power from anti-Western elements. Everywhere else, it was Mr. Richards' task to explain the new policy and invite governments to approve it. The general response was overwhelmingly favorable. No country was called upon to enter into treaty obligations with the United States. All that was required was an expression of its government's attitude to the Doctrine, and it was naturally desired that this attitude be as affirmative as possible. Israel was caught again in her inescapable dilemma. The Government had pledged itself, on taking office in the autumn of 1955, not to associate itself with "any aggressive purpose or alliance directed against any Power whatsoever." It was now not being asked to join an alliance nor did it regard the purpose of the Eisenhower Doctrine as aggressive. But a fear was felt by many—and specifically by two Socialist parties, Mapam and Leachdut Haavoda, which formed part of the Government coalition—that the Soviet Union was not likely to take so indulgent a view. In the end, after nearly three weeks of drafting and redrafting, the Government defined its attitude in a statement issued on May 21, 1957:

> The Government of Israel welcomes the support of the United States for the preservation of the independence of Middle Eastern states and for the development of economic strength dedicated to the maintenance of their independence.

In the course of [the conversations with Ambassador Richards] the Government of Israel reaffirmed its adherence to the following principles which, it is confident, also command the sympathy and support of the United States:

1. Israel reaffirms that in the conduct of its international relations it is guided by the principles and purposes of the Charter of the United Nations to strengthen universal peace, to develop friendly relations among nations, to settle international disputes by peaceful means, and to achieve international co-operation in the economic, social and humanitarian spheres.

2. In conformity with its obligations under the Charter, it is opposed to aggression from any quarter against the territorial integrity and political independence of any country. It entertains no aggressive intent against any other people or nation anywhere, and is agreed on the importance of preserving the political independence and territorial integrity of the countries of the Middle East.

3. It recognizes that every effort must be made to achieve lasting peace both in the Middle East and throughout the world and will co-operate with the United States and other friendly governments to this end.

4. It recognizes that for the promotion of stability, well-being and peace in the Middle East it is vital to promote economic development dedicated to the strengthening of national independence.

5. The Government of Israel expresses its appreciation of the interest shown and assistance rendered over many years in the development of the State of Israel by the Government and people of the United States.

The United States, in a communiqué published the same day, "noted the statement made by the Government of Israel . . . in which that Government expressed its support of the purposes of the Middle East policy set forth by President Eisenhower . . . The United States shares and supports the principles and objectives outlined in Israel's statement relating to the American policy under the Doctrine."

There was scarcely a word in Israel's statement to which the Soviet Union could take exception. It explicitly abjured aggression and aggressive intent. There was an eloquent omission of any reference to "international communism." All the emphasis was on peace, co-operation, national independence and loyalty to the Charter of the United Nations. But the statement was of course made in relation to the Eisenhower Doctrine, and not *in vacuo*. The United States was entitled to see in it the "support of the purposes" of the Doctrine which Israel had been encouraged to express. For the first time, Israel was associated, however subtly, with the objects of American policy in the Middle East. The dilemma, however, was not resolved. Mapam and Leachdut Haavoda, traditionally suspicious of American aims, had voted, in the Cabinet, against the Government's statement. But in Israel, as elsewhere, the principle of collective Cabinet responsibility is sacred; in addition to the reasons valid for democracy in general, all government in Israel has from the start been by coalition and would not be workable at all if the principle were not rigorously applied. If the two parties had voted against the statement when it was brought before the Knesset for approval on June 3, 1957, they would have had to withdraw from the Government, which would then have had to be reconstituted on a new basis, further to the right. In the end, they abstained— after it had been agreed in advance that by this action they would not forfeit their membership in the Government. Only the five Communist members opposed the statement. Out of a House of 120 members, fifty-nine voted for the Government and thirty-nine abstained. The abstainers included the right-wing opposition which, for all its support of the Eisenhower Doctrine, would not support the Government.

The episode showed, as had been shown often before, how deeply an issue of foreign policy could stir Israel. It was certainly a worthy occasion, the *dénouement* of a drama that had been playing on the national stage for nine years. There was something in it, in reflection, of the ideological struggle which had rent the world. There was a profound difference of opinion how best to safeguard Israel's security and independence. Foremost in all minds, characteristically, were the heartsearching and anxiety about the future of Soviet Jewry. It was not by accident that Mr. Ben Gurion, in the Knesset debate, built his peroration round this theme. Israel, he said, was in one respect unique among the nations of the world: it was a state whose supreme ideal was the "ingathering of the exiles." It was natural for Israel to cultivate close ties with countries which helped to promote her development and enabled their Jewish communities to share in her upbuilding. Foremost among these countries was the United States. But this did not exclude, "nor should it in any degree diminish," the maintenance of normal relations with any other country. Israel had declared that she harbored no aggressive designs against anyone and had not denounced any other country:

> The democratic regime and basic human freedoms in Israel are the rock foundations of our state; but we do not see any need, nor indeed feel that we have any right, to interfere in the internal regime of any other country. Our only desire is to create international conditions which will strengthen our security and will assist us in realizing Israel's supreme ideal: the absorption of immigrants.

Mr. Ben Gurion had devoted the opening parts of his speech to the Arab states, whose "hostile designs . . . are sustained by the open and constant support of mighty world forces, which incessantly slander Israel and incite against her, at the same time providing ever increasing military assistance to her enemies." The controversy over the Eisenhower Doctrine embraced all the elements which from the beginning had complicated the definition of Israel's foreign policy. They complicate it still and are likely to complicate it for years to come. The security of Israel and the security of the Jewish people are closely intertwined. Both are profoundly affected by the East-West conflict, particularly as it manifests itself in the Middle East. They are menaced by Arab hostility, which thrives in a world divided between East and West. If ever a country had a vital interest in world peace, that country is Israel. She lies at what Mr. Dean Acheson has called "a crossroads of power." Her neighbors in this strategic area are united against her. Whichever way she turns, there are dangers. The Eisenhower Doctrine provided her, for the first time, with hope of aid against some of these dangers.

The Soviet Union had reacted to the Eisenhower Doctrine long before it reached the stage of Congressional endorsement. On February 11, 1957, the Soviet Foreign Minister, in identical notes handed at Moscow to the representatives of the United States, Great Britain and France, initiated a correspondence which was to continue for months. The peoples of the Middle East were not to be allowed to forget that the Great Powers presided over their destinies. If the Powers were careful each to abjure any thought of interfering in the affairs of individual Middle Eastern states, their notes made it clear that the affairs of the Middle East as a whole were of concern to them all. The Soviet Union explicitly based its interest in Middle Eastern peace on the fact, among others, that the area was situated in direct proximity to its own borders.

Mr. Shepilov's note attributed the crisis in the Near and

Middle East mainly to the fact that "it is still intended to use—without the consent of the United Nations and in a unilateral manner—the armed forces of one of the Great Powers . . . in order to interfere in the internal affairs of this region." With this it bracketed that Power's offer to provide economic aid for the countries of the region, "along with the imposition upon them of conditions by which these countries are to renounce any ties with certain countries which are members of the United Nations." The note went on to say that "the afore-mentioned plan"—the Eisenhower Doctrine—was nothing but "a continuation of a policy of isolated, aggressive military blocs such as NATO, SEATO and the Baghdad Pact, and the setting up of artificial economic and political barriers inter-fering with normal relations between states." At the basis of the policy of the Soviet Union, on the other hand, lay the principle of peaceful co-existence of states, "irrespective of differences in their social or state system." It was a known fact that "in establishing its friendly relations with the Arab coun-tries, the Soviet Union not only did not seek any deterioration in the relations of those countries with other Great Powers, but on the contrary upheld the need for broad international co-operation, and the need to ensure stable peace and the creation of an atmosphere of trust in the area of the Near and Middle East." The Soviet Union, forswearing all desire to possess military bases or concessions of any kind, believed that the need to strengthen peace and security in the Near and Middle East demanded joint action by the Great Powers, "this being particularly in accord with the United Nations Charter." It accordingly proposed a number of principles, to be made the basis of a declaration by the four Powers, "the adoption of which would exclude the possibility of any dangerous, uni-lateral action by this or that Great Power."

The proposed declaration began with a lengthy preamble, by which the signatories, among other things, would "acknowledge and respect the lofty principles of relations between states formulated at the Bandung conference of Asian and African countries" and "recognize the need for a peaceful settlement of all outstanding international problems and questions relating to the Near and Middle East by way of negotiations." It concluded by propounding the six principles which the Powers were to pledge themselves to follow:

1. The preservation of peace in the Near and Middle East by settling questions at issue exclusively by peaceful means, on the basis of the method of negotiations.

2. Noninterference in the internal affairs of the countries of the Near and Middle East. Respect for the sovereignty and independence of these countries.

3. Refusal to undertake any attempt to draw these countries into military alignments with the participation of the Great Powers.

4. The liquidation of foreign bases and the withdrawal of foreign troops from the territory of countries of the Near and Middle East.

5. Joint refusal to supply arms to countries of the Near and Middle East.

6. Assistance in the economic development of countries of the Near and Middle East, without putting forward any political, military or other conditions incompatible with the dignity and sovereignty of these countries.

Nowhere in the note or in the draft declaration was Israel mentioned by name. Apart from the pointed reference to the Soviet Union's friendly relations with the Arab states, the note spoke throughout in terms of "the Near and Middle East." It must be supposed that this meant the same as "the general area of the Middle East," from Karachi to Rabat, covered by the Congressional resolution on the Eisenhower Doctrine.

The Western Powers, after consultation among themselves, drafted separate replies, but they demonstrated their solidarity by delivering them on the same day, exactly one month later. The three notes of March 11 followed similar lines; the main differences between them lay in the fact that Britain alone of the Western Powers had signed the Baghdad Pact and accordingly took it upon herself to expound its objectives, while the United States was concerned especially to refute the Soviet Union's charges against the Eisenhower Doctrine.

The United States stressed that it adhered and would continue to adhere to the principles of the United Nations Charter in its dealings with the countries of the Middle East, "as elsewhere." It fully supported, together with the other principles of the Charter, those singled out in the Soviet note: peaceful settlement of disputes, noninterference in the internal affairs of other countries and respect for their sovereignty and independence. It felt obliged, however, to point out that the Soviet Union could demonstrate its own willingness to carry out these high principles "by itself respecting those UN resolutions addressed to the U.S.S.R. calling for compliance by the U.S.S.R., such as those relating to its actions with respect to Hungary." After this reminder that the world crisis was not confined to the Middle East, the United States note went on:

> The form which co-operation in the Middle East should take—with specific reference to the proposal of the Soviet Government—is a matter for decision in consultation with the Middle Eastern states. Because of its respect for the principle of noninterference in the affairs of other nations, the United States would not wish to be party to an attempt by the Great Powers, as suggested by the U.S.S.R., to arrogate to themselves decisions on matters of vital importance to the nations of the Middle East; or to prevent those who feel themselves threat-

ened from associating of their own free will with other nations in legitimate collective security arrangements, in accordance with the provisions of the United Nations Charter.

While the United States had consistently recognized a need on the part of the Middle Eastern states to maintain a certain level of armed forces to assure their internal security and legitimate self-defense, and to play their part in the defense of the area as a whole, it had as consistently sought to avoid an arms race between the Arab states and Israel. It therefore regretted that the Soviet Government had seen fit to effect massive shipments of arms into the area at a time when regional disputes there had become sharply exacerbated.

The Soviet proposal, the note continued, was clearly based on a false premise, deriving presumably from a distorted interpretation of United States policies. President Eisenhower's outline of United States policy toward the Middle East envisaged genuine practical efforts designed to consolidate peace and security there in full co-operation with the countries concerned. There was cause for considerable doubt as to the seriousness of the Soviet Government's invitation to the United States to join it in co-operation in the Middle East. The invitation had been put forward at a time "when certain Soviet official acts and statements suggest that the U.S.S.R. neither desires nor expects such co-operation." The United States "would like to be able to hope" that the Soviet Union would make its own contribution to tranquillity in the Middle East. It naturally desired to see friendly relations between the states there, but also between them and countries outside the area, including the Soviet Union. However, as elsewhere, this depended largely on the Soviet Union itself: "if the U.S.S.R. will indeed conduct itself in a manner conforming to the principles it proposes, it will be moving in this direction and not only make a contribution to peace in the Middle East, but in other areas as well."

The British and French notes similarly doubted the good faith of the Soviet Union, whose actions in Hungary could be regarded as compatible neither with the decisions of the United Nations nor with the principle of noninterference in the affairs of other countries. France believed that the solution of the Middle Eastern crisis depended on a "concrete and persevering effort" to resolve existing difficulties, particularly as concerned the Israel-Arab problem and freedom of navigation in the Suez Canal. She also singled out for mention the problem of the Arab refugees. Great Britain, while agreeing with some of the features of the Soviet proposal, regretted their presentation "in the context of unwarranted attacks on Her Majesty's Government and their allies" and felt that this background must inevitably create doubt whether they were intended as a serious contribution toward their professed aims. The massive shipments of Soviet arms into the Middle East had served only to accentuate tension and had, indeed, set in train a chain of developments which aggravated existing disputes and brought further misfortunes to an already troubled area, "not least to the recipients of the arms themselves." It had been Britain's consistent policy to avoid an arms race between Israel and the Arab states—here the British and American notes used almost identical terms. As for the Baghdad Pact, it was consistent with Article 51 of the United Nations Charter and, moreover, contained a specific undertaking by the parties to refrain from interference in one another's internal affairs. It was the Soviet Union and its propaganda organs which had "for long sought not only to sharpen and perpetuate differences between countries but also to subvert the loyalty of local populations towards their established Governments." Britain could not be party to proposals, such as those made by the Soviet Government, which tended to impose on the countries of the Near and Middle East "restrictions on their sovereignty and foreign policy of a kind not accepted by countries in Europe and elsewhere." The object of promoting the peace, prosperity and independence of the states concerned would not be furthered by the issuance of the declaration proposed by the Soviet Government, about which these states "would not have been consulted and in which they are not being invited to participate."

It was over a month before the Soviet Union returned to the charge. On April 19, 1957, it addressed separate notes to the United States, Great Britain and France. This time the texts were not identical. This time, too, Israel, which had been mentioned in one context or another by each of the Western Powers in its reply to the original Soviet note, figured prominently in the Soviet argument.

Attacking American membership in the Military Committee of the Baghdad Pact, the Soviet Government declared that the diplomatic moves which the United States had been making in the Middle East did not square with the statement that it took the principles of the United Nations Charter as a guide for its relations with the countries of the area. The Eisenhower Doctrine provided for the dispatch of American armed forces to these countries. It was clear that the responsibility for the exacerbated situation in the Middle East lay with the Governments of the Western Powers, "the Government of the United States included." For a number of years, the Soviet note alleged, the United States had been supplying arms "in large consignments" to Israel and the countries of the Baghdad Pact. It was the arms supplied by the United States and other Western Powers which had given rise to an arms race and had made possible "the armed attack on Egypt by Israel in co-operation with Britain and France." As regards the arms purchases made by some of the Arab states "in the countries outside the Atlantic bloc," in these cases the Arab states concerned had exercised their legal sovereign rights in taking the necessary steps to meet their defense and security requirements.

After rejecting reference to "the so-called Hungarian question" as irrelevant, the Soviet note went on:

> The situation in the Middle East . . . has lately been growing more and more tense owing to the steps taken unilaterally by the Western Powers. Israeli statesmen's provocative declarations addressed to Egypt are causing a most unsettled situation in the Middle East. The Soviet Government has emphatically denounced such declarations as well as the efforts of some Powers to make Israel initiate another dangerous act of provocation against Egypt and other Arab states. There is no reason to doubt that if the United States Government denounced Israel's aggressive designs, this would contribute in large measure toward normalizing the situation in the Middle East.

The United States, by declining the principles of the declaration which the Soviet Union had proposed, and by making no constructive proposals of its own, was in fact refusing to search for an acceptable basis for the settlement of the disputed issues of the Middle East. The Soviet Government now proposed that the four Powers should at least join in a declaration condemning the use of force in the settlement of the unresolved problems of the area, as contrary to the principles of the United Nations Charter.

The notes to Great Britain and France followed the same general pattern, but they dealt more specifically with the points raised in the British and French replies to the first Soviet note. France, in particular, was called to account for her friendly relations with Israel. The Soviet Union regarded France's rejection of the proposed quadripartite declaration as

all the more regrettable since the situation in the Middle East . . . remains very tense and fraught with dangerous new complications. It is well known that Israel, acting as she is in defiance of the relevant decisions of the United Nations, is openly threatening to restart aggression against Egypt if her claims are not met. In so doing, Israel is making no secret of the fact that she counts on support from certain quarters of the Western Powers. Nor can one overlook Western press reports to the effect that the French Government's official spokesmen have promised Israel economic and military assistance in the event of action by her against Egypt. The concentration of air forces on Cyprus appears to be linked with these plans.

The note recalled that at the talks with French ministers in Moscow in May 1956 "both Governments agreed . . . to support the initiative of the United Nations in ensuring a peaceful settlement of disputes between the Arab states and Israel on a basis acceptable to the parties concerned. However . . . the French Government has chosen a different line of action inconsistent with the principles of the United Nations."

It was by now clear that the Soviet Union had cast Israel finally for the part of stooge to the Western Powers. Israel had no alliance with any one of these Powers, but this was to make no difference. The members of the Baghdad Pact, though allied individually with the United States and collectively with Great Britain, were not accorded the distinction of separate mention in the Soviet note. Iraq, for example, despite her rupture of diplomatic relations with the Soviet Union two years before, was regarded as still capable of redemption by virtue of her being an Arab state. Her central part in the Baghdad Pact was but a venial sin; Israel's was mortal.

The Western Powers once more consulted among themselves and allowed almost two months to pass before replying to the second Soviet note. Their replies, again not identical, were described by the State Department as "parallel."

The United States, in its reply of June 12, considered that a declaration condemning the use of force was unnecessary. Opposition to the use of force in the settlement of disputes anywhere had been and continued to be a cardinal element of its foreign policy. The principle was also embodied in the United Nations Charter, to which the four Powers had all adhered:

> Rather than a repetition of existing obligations, what is necessary is loyal implementation of the principles of the Charter. It was this conviction—not, as the Soviet Government alleges, a desire to divert attention from serious solutions of Middle Eastern problems—which prompted the United States Government to refer to Hungary in its Note of March 11.

Noting the Soviet Union's assertion that its concern over conditions in the Middle East arose from its own proximity to the area, the United States observed that "it is just those countries lying closest to the Soviet Union which have been most vigorously attacked in the recent Soviet campaign of threat and intimidation aimed at the legitimate efforts for self-defense undertaken by the nations in question." Public attacks upon the Governments of these states, together with subversive intervention in their domestic affairs, gave them good cause to seek the strengthening of their security, as certain states in the Middle East were now doing in concert with one another. The Soviet Government, the note concluded, could contribute toward the establishment of peace and security in the Middle East by working constructively within the United Nations for the solution of fundamental problems in the area, "among which the Arab-Israeli dispute is outstanding."

The British note, delivered on June 7, rejected as unfounded the Soviet Government's suggestions that the Western Powers had over the years favored one side or the other in the "Palestine dispute" with regard to arms deliveries. Her Majesty's Government understood the Soviet Government's concern with regard to the security of the Soviet Union, but "other countries have an equal concern with their own security." It was this concern which had prompted the member states of the Baghdad Pact to undertake, as free and equal partners, the joint measures necessary to protect themselves against any possible aggressive expansion and to "co-operate together" for their mutual security and well-being. They did not see why the Soviet Union should question the steps they took in the interests of their own security. The Baghdad Pact was purely defensive; its members had no aggressive intentions whatever against the Soviet Union or any other country. In concluding, the British note laid its main emphasis on the Soviet Government's attitude toward Arab-Israel relations:

> If the Soviet Government are seriously concerned about the possibility of hostilities in the Middle East, they will agree that it is important to define the main focus of tension which is likely to lead to such hostilities. As a result of the interest they have recently shown in the Middle East and from their study of its problems, they cannot have failed to perceive that the main focus of tension, in fact, lies in the Arab-Israel dispute. The other factors mentioned in the Soviet Note are either subsidiary or irrelevant, and it is the continuance of the Arab-Israel dispute which makes it impossible to achieve

lasting peace, stability and prosperity in the area. In the opinion of Her Majesty's Government any effective contribution by the Soviet Government towards the relaxation of tension in the Middle East, which they profess to desire, must be directed to the central problem of the above-mentioned dispute. The Soviet Government have so far made no constructive and realistic proposals in this respect and have apparently preferred to make vague generalizations and accusations regarding the alleged intentions of Governments outside the area. If the Soviet Government were to provide concrete evidence that their actions, for instance in the Security Council of the United Nations, would be along the lines indicated above, this would certainly be welcomed by Her Majesty's Government.

It is not known how the Soviet Government reacted to the tone of this communication, but it must have been evident at Moscow that a determined effort was being made here to divert attention from the Baghdad Pact, of which Britain was a member, and concentrate it on the problem of Israel and the Arab states. The Soviet Union had not been alone in failing to make "constructive and realistic proposals" for its solution.

The French Government, in its reply of June 11, also referred, in a sentence, to Israel-Arab relations as the main source of tension in the Middle East. It denied absolutely that France had promised Israel economic and military assistance in the event of renewed action by her against Egypt and declared that the Soviet Government's allusion to the concentration of French air forces on Cyprus was wholly without foundation. As for Hungary, "the Soviet Government is certainly aware itself of the contradiction which exists between its two policies, the European and Arab, as far as concerns the right of nations to manage their own affairs freely and the tasks which fall to the United Nations in safeguarding this right."

France attached particular importance to the question of free navigation in the Suez Canal and regretted the completely negative attitude which the Soviet Union had adopted on this question at the last meeting of the Security Council.

There the correspondence rested—until it was resumed almost three months later. On September 3, 1957, the Soviet Government again addressed notes to the three Western Powers. They brought the subject up to date by referring to events in Oman and Yemen, but otherwise they had little to add. The disputants had had their say, and they could say no more without repeating themselves *ad nauseam*. Each had been at pains to throw off the reproach of interference in the domestic affairs of other countries—and to fasten it on the other side. Metaphysically, this was the central motif of the argument and perhaps no more unreal than most of the rest of it. It could not be expected that the two sides which faced one another in the cold war would reach agreement on the Middle East by correspondence, and it is clear that neither side expected to. It was significant that in their last round of replies not one of the Western Powers came to Israel's defense. France was concerned to refute the allegations which the Soviet Union had made against her in connection with Israel, but her note made no reference to the Soviet charge that Israel was "openly threatening to restart aggression against Egypt." The United States did not react to the Soviet Union's allegations about "the efforts of some Powers to make Israel initiate another dangerous act of provocation against Egypt and other Arab states" nor to the invitation to denounce Israel's "aggressive designs." The Western Powers may have decided, in consultation with one another, to treat the Soviet Government's charges against Israel with the contempt they believed such charges deserved. On the other hand, the studied silence in which they passed over them may have been their way of disowning responsibility for anything Israel might say or do, and so repudiating the allegation that Israel was their tool. As if to emphasize the point, the United States countered the Soviet Government's delivery of arms to Syria and Egypt by speeding up its own deliveries to Jordan, Saudi Arabia and Iraq.

Events were soon to show that, if this was indeed the intention, the Soviet Union was not willing to respect it. In the following months, Soviet accusations that Israel was operating as the instrument of the Western Powers, and of the United States in particular, were pressed more and more strongly. For weeks on end they formed one of the main ingredients of the propaganda dished out by press and radio. Not a day was to pass without its attack on Israel. By July 8, 1957, Moscow radio was accusing Israel of "constantly carrying out provocative attacks on Syrian frontier posts, in accordance with plans worked out in Washington." Four days later an article appeared in *Sovietski Flot*:

The American imperialists and their partners in the aggressive plots in the Middle East are again trying to exploit Israel as an instrument in the war against the independence of Arab countries . . . The United States is providing Israel with arms and military supplies to the value of $96,000,000 . . . The United States is helping Israel to set up military camps on the Syrian frontier, in areas from which it is planned to carry out aggressive operations against Syria. Military equipment is reaching the demilitarized zone between Israel and Syria at a rapid rate. The aggressive circles of Israel are working out, with the support of the United States, plans for a military assault on Syria. With the knowledge of Washington, Israeli forces are being concentrated on the Syrian frontier and frequently open fire on the Syrian frontier patrols. By means of these provocations, the American imperialists are aiming to draw Syria and Egypt into war with Israel, in order then to intervene by military force in their domestic affairs.

The technique was always the same: to repeat a single idea over and over again, in the hope that a slight variation in wording would somehow lend verisimilitude to the statement as a whole. Soviet propaganda agencies now "discovered" French forces in the demilitarized zone, waiting with their Israeli comrades-in-arms to pounce on Syria.* Soon the technique was refined. The Egyptian and Syrian press began to copy, almost word for word, what was said or printed in the Soviet Union. The Soviet press and radio would then quote these statements on Egyptian and Syrian authority, as news or views attributed to the best-informed sources. In August the Institute of Oriental Studies at Moscow, a branch of the Soviet Academy of Sciences, published the first number of a new monthly, *Sovremienny Vostok*, "The Contemporary East," which plunged straight into the subject of Israel:

> The Government of Israel . . . has confirmed its readiness to play the part of arsonist for American imperialist policy in the Near and Middle East. . . . In accepting the Eisenhower Doctrine, with all the results that flow from it, the ruling circles of Israel have intensified their provocations against the neighboring Arab countries . . . Israel is persisting with the

---

* There were, in fact, no Israeli troops there, let alone French. This was, however, not the first time in history that Syria was under an illusion that Israel, reinforced by foreign allies, was about to attack her. *Cf.* II Kings, vii, 6: "For the Lord had made the host of the Syrians to hear a noise of chariots, and a noise of horses, even the noise of a great host: and they said one to another, Lo, the king of Israel hath hired against us the kings of the Hittites, and the kings of the Egyptians, to come upon us." Little had changed since the days of Jehoram, the son of Ahab, except that now it needed only a human agency to conjure up the imaginary enemy force.

line of new provocations and keeping up the tension in the Near and Middle East. It is no secret to anyone that Israel is pursuing this policy at the dictation of Washington . . . In connection with this, the Egyptian newspaper *Ash-Sha'ab* writes that the United States is inciting Israel to provocative actions against Egypt, for the single purpose of "causing a crisis and creating complications in this part of the world" . . . It is clear to everyone that the American imperialists, in foisting the Eisenhower Doctrine on Israel, are striving to bring about a new dispute in the Near and Middle East.

These attacks on Israel served as cover for the consolidation of Soviet influence in Syria and Egypt. They were not confined to characterizing Israel, for the enlightenment of the rest of the world, as the stooge of American imperialism, or to accusing her of provocative designs against her neighbors. From time to time a direct warning would be addressed to the Israel Government. The article in *Sovremienny Vostok*, concluding that Israel had embarked on "a path pregnant with dangerous results for herself," struck the same minatory note which had been the *clou* of Marshal Bulganin's letters to Mr. Ben Gurion nine months before.

Israel had no means of defending herself against these charges, except to reject them as vituperative and untrue; nor did the Western Powers rush to her aid. It was perhaps sufficient that the credit of the Soviet press and radio did not stand high, and that anyone who cared to check the facts would find out at once that they were without foundation. When Soviet propaganda alleged that the Israel Government had evacuated the entire population of Eilat prior to handing over the port to the United States as a military base, the local mayor invited the Tass correspondent at Tel Aviv to fly down and see for himself. The invitation was refused—the correspondent's wife was having a baby. When United Nations observers scoured every inch of the demilitarized zone and found no troops, not even the French whom Soviet newspapers had been reporting, the story was brought to a hasty end. The Soviet press blandly congratulated itself on having exposed the aggressive designs of the United States and having left Israel and France with no choice but to withdraw their forces. No wonder there were none there when the United Nations men came round to look!

This device, familiar from other theaters of the cold war, served as a sharp reminder to Israel that she must not lose sight of the new realities being created around her. The knowledge that these realities affected the whole of the Middle East, and not Israel alone, did little to ease her situation. For one thing, they affected her far more harshly than they did any other country in the area. For another, she could not huddle up for warmth against her neighbors; from every quarter the winds blew cold.

8

Israel in Asia

THE ASIAN NATIONS did not welcome the birth of Israel. The resolution presented to the United Nations General Assembly on November 29, 1947, recommended formally the partition of Palestine and the establishment there of two independent states, one Jewish and one Arab. But powerful Arab opposition had narrowed—and perhaps simplified—the issue. Delegations were, in fact, voting for or against the establishment of a Jewish state. Of the seven Asian countries which at that time were members of the United Nations, only one—the Philippines—voted in favor. Four—Afghanistan, India, Iran and Pakistan—voted against; of these, three were wholly Moslem, while the fourth, India, was obsessed by the problem of a Mos-

lem minority forty million strong. China abstained. The dele-
gate of Thailand was not present when the vote was taken.
The picture could not have been clearer, and this was before
Bandung.

After Israel came into existence, the Asian countries hesi-
tated to grant her recognition. Almost a year passed before
China, the Philippines and, obliquely, Ceylon recognized her.
They were followed by Burma in December 1949, and by
India and Thailand in the autumn of the following year.
There was no rush to accept the new sister-nation which had
achieved independence on the Asian continent.

Yet it was by no accident that the Jewish state was established
on the continent of Asia. It represented the living embodi-
ment of one of Asia's oldest cultures, which the Jewish people
had carried with them, and spread, during the two thousand
years of their wandering. Israel stood for the revival of this
culture, which was as much a national or popular culture as
that of India or Burma or the Arabs. It was, however, a culture
about which the rest of Asia knew little or nothing, and of
whose existence it was barely conscious. Apart from the Jewish
communities of Yemen, Iraq and Iran, Jews were spread thinly
in Asia. The Jews of India were so few as scarcely to invite
notice. Elsewhere they were mostly recent immigrants, regarded as Baghdadis or Europeans.

Israel's early difficulties in securing acceptance by the other
countries of Asia derived largely from ignorance and incomprehension. The Jewish national movement, in the fifty years
of its struggle for political independence, had concentrated,
inevitably, on Europe and America. It had had little need or
occasion for contacts with Asia. The early pioneers came
mostly from Europe. Political, economic and moral support
came from the Jews of Europe and America; there were none
in Asia from whom such support could be looked for. The
League of Nations had conferred the Palestine mandate on

Great Britain, with the result that the political headquarters of the movement, outside Palestine, was established in London. The Permanent Mandates Commission of the League of Nations only once had an Asian member. The Zionist leaders were rarely called upon, or given an opportunity, to explain their aims to an Asian country, nor was any Asian country called upon to hear them.

Incomprehension led easily to prejudice. Since Great Britain held the mandate for Palestine, the Jewish national movement was represented, and resented, as a partner or tool of British imperialism. As such, it was bound to offend the susceptibilities, and invite the opposition, of almost all Asia. Jawaharlal Nehru, in one of the letters he wrote to his daughter from prison,* accepted the view that Zionism was "an accomplice of British imperialism." (Gandhi thought that the Jews of Palestine could find "hundreds of ways of reasoning with the Arabs, if they will only discard the help of the British bayonet." His advice to them was characteristic: "They can offer Satyagraha in front of the Arabs and offer themselves to be shot or thrown into the Dead Sea without raising a little finger against them.") † It is likely that even now some such prejudice lingers in Mr. Nehru's mind. For too many Asians, including political and intellectual leaders, the connection of Israel with the western extremity of their continent begins with the Balfour Declaration of 1917.

The Arabs, for their part, have increasingly exploited the slogan of "imperialism" or "colonialism" against Israel; the Bandung Conference taught them its power. Israel alone among the nations of Asia has never received credit for her emancipation from colonial tutelage. Her struggle for political independence, carried on against the mandatory Power

---

* *Glimpses of World History,* revised edition (London, 1939), pp. 762–65.

† *Harijan,* November 26, 1938.

for years, has never been seen in the same light as the parallel struggle of the Indians, the Arabs or the Burmese. Had contact in the years of revolt been closer, there would have been greater comprehension, both before and after independence was attained. As it was, Asia failed to see Israel as a people fighting desperately for its national resurgence. In the Arab war against Israel in 1948, Asian sympathies were almost wholly on the Arab side.

In a demographic sense, Israel is of course not wholly Asian, nor even mainly; her population today is 40 per cent Asian and African in origin, and 60 per cent European. (In the seven years from 1950 to 1956, exactly 30 per cent of the new immigrants came from Europe, 31.6 per cent from Africa, 36.9 per cent from Asia.) The people of Israel have come together from every part of the world, bringing with them, with their own traditions, the ways of the countries in which they or their parents were born and bred. Hundreds of thousands have come from Asia—from Yemen, Iran, Iraq, Syria, India, Afghanistan —and almost equal numbers from the Arabic-speaking territories of North Africa. But the pattern of national life was set by the early pilgrims and pioneers and has remained essentially European. Israel lies at the junction of Asia, Africa and Europe; no single continent can, except technically, claim her. By a strange irony, it is what Israel has brought from the West that attracts Asian students and experts. During the past ten years Israel has played host to visitors and delegations from every part of Asia, including government officials from many countries, who have come to study co-operation in agriculture, new methods of social work and other subjects in which Israel has something of special value to show. The same Government of India which cannot bring itself to establish diplomatic relations with Israel has not hesitated to send delegations to study her diverse forms of collective and co-operative farming.

One further circumstance has made it more difficult for

Asians than for others to understand Israel. The very name "Israel" is part of the Christian heritage and, as such, part of Western culture. In France, in Poland, in Peru, in Australia— hardly anywhere outside Asia can a child grow up in a civilized community without learning of Israel. The Holy Land is a universal concept, even for those who are not devoutly religious. Jerusalem, Nazareth, Galilee are household names, with Carmel, Gilboa, Capernaum but a shade less familiar. When the Jewish state was established and called Israel, it did not have to explain itself—except in Asia. Buddhism and Hinduism derived from an entirely separate religious and philosophic tradition. Islam was hostile in any case. It is possible that Israel did not take this sufficiently into account. She did not always realize that in introducing herself to the other nations of Asia it was not enough to present a visiting card inscribed "Israel." It would be necessary to go back to first principles and start, if not from Adam, at least from the Patriarchs and the Exodus.

There was a final obstacle. Asia, which, precisely because it lay outside the Judaeo-Christian tradition, had never known anti-Semitism, could not recognize instinctively the need and justice of a Jewish state.

In her early years Israel made sporadic attempts to seek contact with Asia and achieve a better understanding. She herself knew scarcely more about Asia than Asia did about her, and for the same reasons. India at that time, and Jawaharlal Nehru personally, exercised a decisive influence in Asia. It was accordingly to India that Israel turned.

In February and March 1952 conversations were held at New Delhi with Pandit Nehru and senior officials of his Ministry of External Affairs. On the lower level, officials pleaded difficulties of finance and personnel as an obstacle to the establishment of diplomatic relations, but it soon became clear that the true reasons lay deeper. On the merits of the case Mr.

Nehru had no doubts. India had recognized Israel over a year before, and it was not logical to balk at diplomatic relations. He was not, at that time, greatly affected by Arab opposition to Israel, though the Syrian minister to India was showing disquiet at these talks with a representative of Israel whom the Indian Government had received with the honors of a state guest. Diplomatic relations with Israel had been held up through the Government's consideration for India's Moslem minority. The problem was presented as one of domestic politics, at least in the main. Indian Moslems had suffered a profound shock by partition. Most of their leaders had left them and gone to Pakistan. Individual Moslems occupied influential positions in India, but the community as a whole was depressed and fearful of the future. The Government had always shown understanding for their situation and had not wanted to heap shock upon shock if it were not absolutely necessary. Mr. Nehru agreed, however, that the question of diplomatic relations should now be reconsidered. Before Israel's representative left New Delhi, he was informed that the Prime Minister had approved the proposal. He was now questioned in detail on housekeeping problems: what was the cost of living in Israel, would it be better for India's minister to buy or rent a house, what were the prospects of hiring servants? A draft budget for the Indian legation was being prepared, though the formal decision to establish diplomatic relations still remained to be confirmed by the Cabinet. This was to be done as soon as the new Government was set up following the elections a few weeks later.

In the end, nothing came of these talks. In January of the following year, one of the Indian officials wrote: "I am distressed to think that the new year has opened without our having a Mission in Israel. I really do not know the reason for this delay." Nobody, in fact, outside Nehru's most intimate circle has ever discovered why the Government of India did not establish diplomatic relations with Israel in the spring or summer of 1952, and no really convincing explanation has been given for its sudden change of mind. So many explanations have been made that it is impossible to tell which, if any, is correct. But there seems little doubt that Moslem hostility to Israel is still the stumbling block—with a shift of emphasis from India's own Moslem minority, which had shown no sign of shock when Nehru recognized Israel in 1950, to Pakistan and the Arab states. Throughout these years Kashmir has affected Indian policy in every field. Mr. Nehru may have feared at one time that if he established relations with Israel, he would throw the Arab states into the arms of Pakistan, their sister in Islam. They might be kept neutral if they believed that their support of Pakistan on Kashmir would lead to India's establishing diplomatic relations with Israel. Such a development would give Israel the entree to the society of Asian nations, and this they were determined at all costs to prevent. If this was, indeed, Mr. Nehru's calculation, he may feel that events have proved him right: the Arab states, more concerned with power than with religious affinities, have in fact never lent Pakistan their full support. Neutralism or "nonalignment" held a powerful appeal for the whole Arab world, and Egypt in particular was happy to be drawn into India's orbit. Mr. Nehru, for his part, was prepared to appease Arab susceptibilities by keeping away from Israel; in practice, he could have established diplomatic relations with Israel without causing more than a flutter of annoyance in Cairo, so deeply dependent has Egypt become on India.

Even before Bandung, Israel's relations with Asia were bedeviled by the Moslem factor, which the Arabs could exploit at will. Many countries of Asia, including some of the most populous and most important, are wholly Moslem. Others have influential Moslem minorities. It was impossible for Israel to break through so solid a wall of prejudice and opposition. Mullahs and muftis, in their appeals to the faithful, denounced dealings with Israel as the Moslem equivalent of mortal sin. The Arab rulers used nationalist arguments which proved no less persuasive. Some of the results have been bizarre. Indonesia will not grant a visa to the holder of an Israeli passport. Pakistan does not accept mail from Israel—nor can you send a letter from Karachi to Tel Aviv.

After the experience of New Delhi, Israel began to look beyond the Moslem world. The first congress of the Asian Socialist Conference met at Rangoon in January 1953. Israel sent a strong delegation, headed by Mr. Moshe Sharett, who was not only one of the leaders of Mapai, the Labor Party of Israel, but also Minister for Foreign Affairs. Mapai was the dominant factor in Israel's coalition Government. The only other Asian country in which a Socialist party was in power was Burma. The links forged at Rangoon between these parties led swiftly to closer relations between the two countries, and later in the year Israel set up a legation in the Burmese capital. As early as 1949, the Government of Burma, in according recognition to Israel, had expressly "looked forward to the establishment of friendly relations." These relations now took shape and have been maintained ever since to the advantage of both countries. Their warmth was strikingly demonstrated when U Nu, the Prime Minister of Burma, visited Israel in the late spring of 1955 and received a triumphal welcome from every section of the people.

Toward the end of 1952 Israel had established her first diplomatic mission in Asia, at Tokyo. Her minister there was subsequently accredited to Thailand as well, just as her ambassador in Rangoon is for reasons of economy accredited also to Laos, the Philippines and Ceylon. In addition to the missions at Tokyo, Rangoon and Colombo, Israel has consular offices at Manila, Bangkok and Bombay. The growth of Israel's representation in Asia has been achieved by degrees, usually in the face of difficulties. These difficulties came to a head at the conference of Asian and African countries which met at Bandung April 18–24, 1954.

Had Israel been invited to take part in the conference, it is unlikely that her delegates could have reached Bandung, since the Indonesian Government would not have given them visas. This was never, however, put to the test, for Israel was not invited.

The Asian-African Conference was open, in theory, to every independent state in Asia and Africa. Indeed, its organizers were anxious to ensure the widest possible representation. But inevitably there were problems. The Republic of China (Formosa) could not be asked, because the People's Republic of China (Peking) was attending. Then there was the question of North and South Korea. In the end, neither was invited— though North and South Vietnam both were, and both came. The Gold Coast was invited, though at that time it had not yet become independent Ghana. Invitations were sent to nine Arab states: Egypt, Iraq, Jordan, Lebanon, Libya, Saudi Arabia, Sudan, Syria and Yemen. Since altogether twenty-nine states attended, the Arabs formed almost one third of the total.

The sponsors of the Bandung Conference were Burma, Ceylon, India, Indonesia and Pakistan. They were faced by the question of whether to invite Israel. When their five Prime Ministers met at Colombo to discuss plans for the conference, U Nu pressed strongly for an invitation to Israel, which he regarded as a matter of course. He was supported by Mr. Nehru. But the Prime Ministers of Indonesia and Pakistan were inflexible in their opposition. To them, Moslems representing Moslem peoples, Israel was an interloper in Asia, an offense to Islam. Neither of their Governments recognized Israel. (In the case of Indonesia there was no validity to this point. Indonesia had won her independence later than Israel, so it was for Israel to recognize *her*—which Israel had, in fact, done.) Above all, the two Prime Ministers had a practical argument: if Israel were invited and came, the Arab states would boycott the conference. Here numbers were a powerful argument, as they have so often been in the United Nations. The Arabs are fond of claiming that they are a single nation, but it is a happy circumstance for them that this single nation is split up into so many independent states. Faced with the choice between one Israel and nine Arab states, those sponsors of the conference who in principle favored Israel's participation found themselves in a dilemma. It was not a question of Ceylon's giving a casting vote to settle the issue. The decision had to be unanimous. In the circumstances it could only be negative, and Israel was not invited. It is certain that the Arabs were bluffing when they threatened to boycott the conference if Israel took part. In similar circumstances, elsewhere, their bluff had been called. But the leaders of the Asian countries, convening a conference which they sensed could be historic, were not prepared to take the risk, even had the Moslems among them allowed it.

Though Israel was not represented, some of the most fiery speeches at the conference were made about her. Her ghost was not unwelcome at the table. Macbeth did not cry avaunt. The Arab members, seizing their chance, fell upon Israel and tore her to pieces—*in absentia*. Other delegates came to Israel's defense, some of the more responsible among them feeling the injustice of attacking a country which was denied the opportunity of presenting its case, quite apart from the insubstantiality of the attacks themselves. But all in all, the Arabs had a field day.

The "Joint Communiqué" of the Asian-African Conference, adopted on the closing day, endorsed a number of principles, most of which were, in fact, inconsistent with Arab policy toward Israel. They included respect for the sovereignty and territorial integrity of all nations, abstention from acts or threats of aggression or the use of force against the territorial integrity or political independence of any country, settlement of all international disputes by peaceful means, and the like. All the Arab delegations supported the adoption of these principles, though they would naturally not understand them to apply to themselves in their dealings with Israel. In addition, the Joint Communiqué contained the following section, under the heading of "Other Problems":

> In view of the existing tension in the Middle East caused by the situation in Palestine, and of the danger of that tension to world peace, the Asian-African Conference declared its support of the rights of the Arab people of Palestine and called for the implementation of the United Nations' resolutions on Palestine and the achievement of the peaceful settlement of the Palestine question.

Nowhere was Israel mentioned by name. Burma, despite her close relations with Israel, found herself constrained, for the sake of Asian-African unity, to accept this declaration. It was, indeed, a watered-down version of the far more peppery text which the Arabs had wished to see adopted. The Arabs did not like its reference to a "peaceful settlement" of their conflict with Israel. But it would have been overweening of them to hope for more than the express "support of the rights of the Arab people of Palestine" to which all Asia and Africa now pledged itself. The reference to "the United Nations' resolutions on Palestine" must be understood as a *terminus technicus*. In the political vocabulary of the Arab states it means only those resolutions which they consider favorable to themselves. It does not include the General Assembly's resolution calling for the establishment of a Jewish state, nor the Security Council's order to Egypt to stop interfering with Israel shipping in the Suez Canal.

The "Middle East resolution" of the Asian-African Conference was interpreted, rightly, as a victory for the Arabs. They proceeded to agitate against Israel all over Asia in the sacred name of Bandung. An "Afro-Asian bloc" in the United Nations had begun to form at the sixth session of the General Assembly in 1951. Bandung gave it firmer shape and strength, and an influence which Arab governments were not slow to enlist in their service. Every matter affecting Israel which comes up at the General Assembly is now discussed by this group before the opening of the public debate. Happily, the Afro-Asian nations do not always see eye to eye with the Arabs. Since 1956, in particular, they have shown an increasing reluctance to be forced into the role of partisans against Israel. Nevertheless, the existence of this bloc, from which Israel despite every consideration of geography remains excluded, is always a potential danger. It says much for the good sense of many Asian governments that, for all the incessant pressure, they have not in fact allowed themselves to be stampeded into automatic support of every Arab cause. Yet Bandung was a blow from which Israel's standing in Asia could not quickly recover.

Another blow soon followed. Israel recognized the People's Republic of China on January 6, 1950, at the same time as India, Great Britain, Norway, Denmark, Finland, Sweden and Switzerland. Quite apart from the fact that she had no special cause for gratitude to the Formosa regime, Israel, in her own recognition policy, made a practice of acknowledging established fact. This was what she had asked of other countries in the early days when she herself was seeking recognition; it was a case of "do as you would be done by." There could be no doubt that the Government of the People's Republic was the effective government of continental China. The domestic political system of China was none of Israel's concern, any more than it was that of Switzerland or Sweden. There was, at that time, no question of diplomatic relations, but Israel always thought of establishing an embassy at Peking as soon as budgetary provision could be made for it. At Bandung, Chou Enlai, representing China, had been temperate in his attitude toward Israel and unenthusiastic about the demands of the Arabs. In February 1955, Israel sent a good-will mission to Peking, headed by Mr. David Hacohen, her minister to Burma. The mission was well received and stayed in China for a month, investigating the possibilities of commercial and diplomatic relations. But soon afterward there came a cooling off on the Chinese side. By this time the understanding between Egypt and the Soviet bloc was under way, to be sealed later in the year by Egypt's arms deal with Czechoslovakia. Keeping in step, Chinese delegations began to visit and woo the Arab states, which still recognized Formosa. In return, Arab commercial and "cultural" delegations traveled to Peking. It was clear that the Government of China had begun to find Israel an embarrassment and decided that she was, for the time being, expendable.

If Israel has not yet fully found her place in the community of Asian nations, it has not been for want of trying. Bandung, and the preliminaries that led up to it, showed that as long as Arab hostility to Israel persists, her path in Asia cannot be easy. In particular, she cannot hope to pierce the armor of Moslem resistance, though here and there it has shown signs of buckling. In the meantime, Israel has been strengthening her relations with Burma, Japan, Ceylon, the Philippines, Thailand and Laos. This is no bad foundation on which to continue building.

As time has passed, the "Bandung spirit," now stepmothered by the Soviet Union, has come increasingly into collision with the realities of the world situation. Despite the eagerness of the Arab states to have the Asian-African Conference convened anew, and to celebrate afresh their triumphs of 1955, there has been no second Bandung.* Not a few governments in Asia and Africa fear that a conference today could be as prolific in embarrassment as in achievement. The growing extremism of Arab thought and action has opened their eyes to the nihilism of the forces with which Israel has had to contend and has shown them Israel's own position and aims in truer perspective. Starting from nothing in 1948, Israel's place in Asia has in ten years, despite all obstacles and opposition, advanced to a point from which progress in future should be less arduous than it has been in the past.

In Africa, apart from the Arab states, the position is not unencouraging. Israel values in particular her ties with Ghana, forged first, like her links with Burma, through a common trade-union and labor interest. Even before Ghana became independent, a consulate of Israel was established at Accra. It was transformed into an embassy three weeks after Ghana's independence became effective in 1957. Ghana students and trainees have come to Israel, and the two countries have growing commercial interests in common. It has become clear that there is a rich field for co-operation between Ghana and Israel, which both Governments are eager to cultivate. A significant step forward was taken in August 1957, when a high-level delegation from Ghana, headed by the Minister of Commerce, Mr. Kojo Botsio, visited Israel. It was met with an enthusi-

---

* An Asian-African "conference" met somewhat rowdily at Cairo at the end of 1957. Described by the Rangoon *Guardian* (January 11, 1958) as "a comedy of leftist agents," it was not representative of the governments of either continent.

asm reminiscent of that which had greeted the Prime Minister of Burma two years earlier.

In the following month, Israel opened an embassy at Monrovia, the capital of Liberia. Liberia had voted for the General Assembly's resolution of November 29, 1947, recommending the establishment of a Jewish state, and had maintained friendly contacts with Israel almost from the first. Here too there is scope for a development of practical relations to serve the interests of both countries.

The position of Ethiopia has been more equivocal. As long as the future of Eritrea was undecided, she felt she could not alienate the Arab states whose votes she needed. After the incorporation of Eritrea into Ethiopia, the situation eased and the Negus became less guarded in his expressions of good will toward Israel. Two representatives of Israel visited him at Addis Ababa early in 1956, and soon afterward a consulate general of Israel was established there, Ethiopia at the same time appointing a consul general at Jerusalem. This put relations between the two countries on an acceptable basis. The real revolution in their relations must come as a result of the opening of the Gulf of Aqaba. There are now regular steamship services direct from Eilat to Massawa; trade and travel between Israel and Ethiopia are no longer dependent on the mercies of Egypt in the Suez Canal.

9

Israel and the Jewish Diaspora

IT IS A COMMONPLACE of our Foreign Service that every Envoy
Extraordinary and Minister Plenipotentiary of Israel has a
dual function. He is Minister Plenipotentiary to the country
to which he is accredited—and Envoy Extraordinary to its
Jews. This has come to be accepted generally—by other governments in the "free" world,* by the Jews of the diaspora,

---

* In most Communist countries contact between diplomatic missions
and the local population is severely restricted. It is impossible for
representatives of Israel to meet Jews freely as they do in other countries. On February 12, 1953, the Soviet Government, in justification of
its rupture of diplomatic relations, declared that "the elementary
conditions for normal activity by the Soviet diplomatic mission are

and by everyone in Israel. It is, in fact, a natural enough situation. King George VI once startled the Chief Rabbi of the Commonwealth by mentioning to him, at a Buckingham Palace reception, that he had the day before received "your ambassador," meaning the ambassador of Israel in London.

In each country the foreign residents constitute what in their circles and in the diplomatic corps is known as a "colony." There is a French colony in Italy, a Swedish colony in Japan, a British colony in Peru. The Jewish community in many countries is seen by gentiles as the Israeli colony. In September 1955, at a climax of the Cyprus crisis, when Jewish property in Istanbul was plundered by anti-Greek rioters, the Turkish Government thought it perfectly natural to instruct its representative at Tel Aviv to express its regrets to the Government of Israel and to assure it that there existed in Turkey "no intention or inclination to prejudice in any way the security or the rights of the Jews of Turkey." The Swiss minister to Brazil once envied his Israeli colleague on the size of his colony; he himself had only 12,000 fellow countrymen—and there were ten times as many Jews.

These colonies can be extremely helpful to their country of origin, and it is one of the duties of every ambassador, minister and consul to keep in close touch with them. The Jews are exceptional, however, and nowhere form a colony in the accepted sense. Members of a Danish colony, for example, are Danish citizens or they may at most, if their own and the local laws allow it, have dual nationality—their Danish nationality of origin and the nationality of the country in which they re-

completely lacking in Israel." Four days later Mr. Ben Gurion replied in the Knesset: "There is no foundation to the contention . . . that conditions for the normal diplomatic functioning of the Soviet Legation do not exist in Israel. This Legation has been assured in our country *a degree of freedom of action that our Legation in Moscow has never dreamed of demanding for itself.*"

side and perhaps were born. Jews in general do not have Israeli nationality; the only Israelis are those who are or have been domiciled in Israel—and the overwhelming majority of Jews in the world have never been to Israel even on a visit. Yet the ties which bind Jews everywhere to Israel are very strong, and Jewish communities abroad are often "colonies" in at least as real a sense as the Germans or Danes or Swiss. Israel does not claim their political allegiance. The Jews are citizens of their own countries, and the question of double loyalty does not arise. But they are bound to Israel by sentiment, and to some extent by self-interest. Exposed as they often are to discrimination, and in many countries fearful for their future, they have felt more secure since Israel came into existence. Just as Americans of Swedish, Irish, English or Italian origin have a "home country" in which they take a pride and an interest even after many generations, Jews all over the world can take a pride and an interest in Israel; and just as Irish Americans and Greek Americans support their "home country," its institutions and villages and their own families, so Jews support Israel, materially and morally.

When Herzl first gave the dream of Jewish independence political shape, he did so in a pamphlet entitled *Der Judenstaat*, "The State of the Jews." He did not call it *Der Jüdische Staat*, "The Jewish State." The difference may seem subtle, but it is real enough. Israel is not merely a state predominantly Jewish in the race, religion or way of life of its people. It is a state for all Jews. The principle was laid down in its Declaration of Independence: "The State of Israel will be open to the immigration of Jews from all countries of their dispersion." Legislative effect was given to this in the Law of Return, passed unanimously by the Knesset on July 5, 1950. Israel is the only country in the world which confers citizenship on an immigrant automatically at the moment he steps off the boat or plane. Every Jew knows that he can migrate to

Israel whenever he feels like it. The gates are always open. At the same time, Israel places no Jew under compulsion to exercise this birthright of his. He is perfectly free, as far as Israel is concerned, to stay where he is. But inevitably a special relationship has sprung up between Israel and Jews everywhere who share the age-old attachment to the Land of Israel. Even if they are unwilling or unable to link their personal lives with it by coming as immigrants, they are animated by a powerful sentiment of solidarity and love. Mr. Ben Gurion, in an Independence Day message in 1957, defined succinctly the links which join Israel and the Jews all over the world:

> The unity of the Jewish people, its sense of a common responsibility for its fate, its attachment to its spiritual heritage, and its love for the nation's ancient homeland, have become more and more intense as a result of the rise of the Third Commonwealth. The ingathering of Israel's exiled and scattered sons is the common task of all sections of the Jewish people wherever they may live. Everything that has been created in this country is the common possession of the Jews of all lands.

Few would quarrel with this definition; it reflects indisputable fact. But it has not been easy to adjust the relationship between Israel and the Jewish communities abroad, particularly in the United States. Before Israel attained political independence, a Jew could either be a Zionist or not. If he was, he believed in Jewish statehood as a political ideal and goal and did his best to help achieve it. If he was not, he would be either indifferent or hostile to the idea, believing it not worth striving for or incapable of realization or, in extreme cases, positively harmful. With the rise of Israel, there had to be a reorientation of attitudes and action. The Zionist's goal was achieved—what was there left for him to do? The non-Zionist

and anti-Zionist found themselves faced with a *fait accompli*—
Israel existed, whether they were interested or pleased or not,
and they were forced to think again.

The adjustment of Jews outside Israel to the reality of Israel has not yet been completed. It is now less a problem of action than of ideas. It was not simply for the sake of talking that
as late as August 1957 an "ideological conference" was called
at Jerusalem and attended by Jewish leaders and thinkers from
all over the world. There is genuine confusion, even distress.
The classical concept of Jewish "exile" presents itself in a new
form. In traditional Jewish thought, reflected in Mr. Ben
Gurion's Independence Day message, the Jewish people had
been in exile since the destruction of the Second Commonwealth in the year 70. The concept of "exile" applied in some
measure even to those who lived in Palestine, for they were
living there under foreign rule. With the establishment of
the Third Commonwealth, Israel, the exile came to an end—
in the sense, at least, that there was again a Jewish state and
that any Jew who wished to return to it was free to do so. It
became natural to distinguish, if not always explicitly, between those Jews who were "at home" or "in their own country"—that is, in Israel as Israeli citizens—and those who
continued to live "in exile," anywhere outside Israel. Instinctively, the majority of Jews accepted this distinction,
though no undue stress was laid on it either in Israel or
abroad; the essential unity of the Jewish people, in terms of
race, tradition and faith, was too strong to brook differentia-
tion along hard and fast lines of any kind.

An ideological crisis arose in the United States, however,
where Jews resented any suggestion that they were living in
"exile." America was their home, Americanism their creed,
the American way of life their heritage. This denial of an
American "exile" implied a break with almost two thousand

years of Jewish thought and teaching. Israeli leaders, steeped in Jewish tradition, found it difficult to adjust themselves to the idea that America was excluded from the "exile," and they continued to think, and sometimes speak, in terms of two Jewish worlds—Israel and the rest. Each time such a thought found expression in speech there would be a protest from American Jewish leaders, deeply sympathetic though they were by nature to Israel and her aspirations. In the end, a *modus vivendi* was achieved. The problem was aired exhaustively in June 1957, when a delegation of the American Jewish Committee, an influential "non-Zionist" group, visited Israel. After much discussion, Mr. Ben Gurion, as Prime Minister of Israel, defined his position in terms which proved acceptable to the Committee's leaders:

> While Israel is open for all Jews who desire or need to come and live in it . . . the State of Israel represents and speaks only on behalf of its own citizens and in no way represents or speaks on behalf of Jews of any other country. The attachment of Jews throughout the world to Israel is based on a joint spiritual and cultural heritage, and on a historical sentiment toward the land which was the birthplace of the Jewish people and of the Book, and which today as the Third Commonwealth of Israel enshrines the regeneration of a people in its ancient homeland and revival of its civilization. Jews throughout the world give expression to this attachment and dedication in various ways. But these, in whatever form they may be expressed, carry no political connotation whatsoever.

This was taken to mean that in Israel's official view American Jews were American citizens, no more and no less, and that they were not necessarily looked upon as children of Israel in exile. Anything they did to express their "attachment

197

and dedication" to Israel, they did as Americans, and not as the detached limb of a foreign state.

Events have robbed the term "Zionism" of much of its original meaning and the old "Zionist movement" of much of its strength.* Mr. Ben Gurion, in his personal capacity, has in recent years made a point of declaring that he is not a Zionist—he is a Jew first, an Israeli second, and that is all. Jews who live outside Israel cannot, in his conception, be partners in Israel's cause, but only "helpers." His attitude has caused some resentment on the part of veteran Zionists who, having devoted their lives to this cause, find they can no longer claim a monopoly of support for Israel. All they can do, differently from others, is to take pride in having been right all along. Support for Israel is now universal among Jews everywhere, apart from a handful of eccentrics. (Here and there one may find a Jew who gives comfort to Abdul Nasser, propagandizing for him actively against Israel, impelled by a form of self-hate which borders on the abnormal.) The fact that so many "Zionists" continue to live in the diaspora has served to blur the distinction between them and other Jews; logic would dictate that Zionists come to Israel to live, but not everyone acts logically. For Israel it is important, indeed vital, that support for her be not confined to any single group. The Jews who in their thousands close their shops and line the streets of Buenos Aires cheering when the ambassador of Israel drives to the Casa Rosada to present his letters of credence may not all have been "Zionists" ten years ago, and the term "Zionist" hardly applies to them now. It is sufficient that today every single one of them takes a pride in Israel, glories in her achievements,

---

* The status of the World Zionist Organization was, after much discussion, defined by law in Israel. Significantly, this law, passed by the Knesset on November 24, 1952, opens with the words: "The State of Israel regards itself as a creation of the whole Jewish people."

worries when things go wrong for her and feels a personal obligation to do whatever he can, financially or otherwise, to help.

Israel has received massive financial support from the Jews of the diaspora. It came to be agreed that the Israeli taxpayer would bear all the normal burden of government expenditure, including defense, thus making Israel responsible for her own budget, like any other state. On the other hand, the costs of immigration would be borne primarily by the diaspora, which had a long tradition of succoring Jews and had for generations financed Jewish rescue and relief work and Jewish migration to every part of the world. In practice, the division of responsibility has worked out rather differently. Israel herself has had to carry an increasing share of the cost of immigration, and particularly of settlement and integration. At the same time, the diaspora has invested large sums in Israel, either directly in industrial enterprises and the like, or through successive bond issues launched in the United States and in countries of Latin America and Western Europe. These loans have gone a long way toward financing Israel's development budgets; the larger the income from them has been, the more Israel herself has been able to divert from development to defense and other urgent domestic needs.

The two-way relationship between Israel and the Jews of the world has a profound significance, politically, materially and morally. It takes up much of the time of all Israel's diplomatic representatives abroad, and most of the time of some. They do their best not to get involved in the internal controversies of local Jewish communities, but they cannot avoid being asked for advice or, when necessary, giving it. At all costs they must refrain from taking sides. In particular, they are careful not to interfere in matters at issue between the Jewish community and the government of the country in which they serve. A Jewish community will sometimes look to them for help of this kind, but it would clearly create an impossible position if the representative of Israel appeared as the protagonist of local Jews in dealings with their governments. Generally speaking, the limitations of an Israeli ambassador in this field are understood and respected, but the latitude he can allow himself in practice will vary. It has happened more than once that a government, on its own initiative, has discussed with the representative of Israel some problem concerning the local Jewish community.* He will normally report to his own Government on important Jewish affairs, particularly when they may affect Israel's interests. He and his staff will be in demand as speakers at Jewish functions and will concern themselves with cultural and educational work. Jews planning investments in Israel will look to the embassy or legation for advice; others will have problems connected with Israeli relatives. All this, with the normal duties of diplomacy, leaves Israel's representatives little time for idling.

The connection between Israel and Jewish communities abroad has affected the Foreign Minister himself. During the eight years in which Mr. Sharett held this office, he traveled far and wide, visiting Jewish communities in North and South America, in Western Europe and in South Africa. At first there was some hesitation, though never on his part. It was asked whether it was possible for the Foreign Minister of one country to go campaigning among the citizens of another—"go campaigning," because no other term adequately conveys

---

* On one occasion, in 1957, the Israel minister in one of the Latin American capitals was requested to call at the Foreign Ministry, where, to his amazement, the Secretary-General began taxing him with some malpractice attributed to a local Jewish citizen. It was only when the minister asked whether the Italian ambassador would have been summoned in similar circumstances affecting a local citizen of Italian extraction that the Secretary-General realized what an anomalous thing he was doing. He had instinctively held Israel responsible for the actions of a Jewish citizen of his own country.

the intensity of these journeyings, with Mr. Sharett meeting Jewish leaders, addressing mass meetings, visiting Jewish schools, helping in financial drives. But it became clear very soon that no one thought this in any way extraordinary—indeed, it was accepted as natural, in nonexilic America as much as elsewhere. For the Jews these were great events—and not only Mr. Sharett's visit to them; every reception by a president, every formal address to a parliament, redounded to the credit of the local community. A pattern was established, to be repeated each year in a different part of the world. When Mrs. Meir became Foreign Minister in 1956 and went to New York for the eleventh and twelfth sessions of the General Assembly, her appearances at Jewish meetings all over the United States were a natural continuation of the tradition established by Mr. Sharett, and of her own past practice as Minister of Labor. The first diffidence had quickly passed, and the task of strengthening relations with the Jews of the world made the same demands on the Foreign Minister as it did on Israel's ambassadors and consuls.

The existence of large Jewish communities abroad has a direct impact on Israel's relations with the countries concerned. The Jews of America, numbering close on six million, are a political factor whose influence may vary but is always felt. The United States is a democracy in which any organized group, sometimes even the smallest, can make its wishes felt and respected. American Jews have never hesitated, as American citizens, to bring their weight to bear in the cause of Israel, though it is hard to say how often, if ever, it has been decisive. Anything they do, they must do of their own free will. Israel cannot employ, command or incite them, though she can, and does, keep them informed of her policies and needs. They work for American friendship with Israel, as Americans of Irish and Italian descent work for friendship with Ireland and Italy. The Jewish community of America is the largest in the world and enjoys proportionate political strength, but Jewish communities play a similar part wherever they are free to maintain their links with Israel.

Such freedom does not exist in the Soviet Union and most other Communist countries. There contact with the outside world is forbidden generally, but the Jews suffer from the ban more than others. The ordinary Russian or Georgian or Rumanian may not feel any deep need for contacts outside, but the Russian, Georgian and Rumanian Jews are drawn to Israel as powerfully as Jews everywhere else and suffer from the deprivation keenly. The establishment of Israel released in the Jews of the Soviet Union an uncontrollable urge for reunion, or at least communication, with the rest of their people. When Israel's first Minister to the U.S.S.R. appeared at the synagogue in Moscow in 1948, there were scenes of messianic frenzy: tens of thousands of Jews packed the streets—it was the first spontaneous, unauthorized demonstration that Moscow had seen since 1917. They knew they were running grave dangers, but their numbers gave them courage. It was a bitter awakening for the Soviet Government, which believed it had destroyed "Zionism" and now saw that thirty years of repression had merely driven it underground into the people's hearts. The Soviet Government began to suspect that by supporting the establishment of Israel it had laid up domestic trouble for itself. If the country's Jews, estimated at three million, were restless before, their restlessness now looked as if it might transport them—who knows how far? The Jews came to be branded as an unreliable, "cosmopolitan" element, and charges of "Zionism" were revived. At least twenty-five prominent Jewish writers and thinkers, arrested in 1948 and the following years, were executed on August 12, 1952. The "doctors' plot" and the Slansky trial in Czechoslovakia followed. No one knows how many "Zionists" are still languishing in Siberian labor camps. To be caught with a Hebrew newspaper is enough to earn a man fifteen years in prison.

This situation has profoundly affected Israel's relations with the U.S.S.R. and other countries of the Soviet bloc. If Israel's gates are open to all Jews, this includes Jews of the Soviet Union. If American Jews do not migrate to Israel because they do not want to, it is one thing; but if Russian Jews cannot come because the Soviet Government does not allow them to, it is another and a very different thing. From Israel's point of view, Soviet Jews enjoy exactly the same right of "return" as all others, and it seems intolerable that they should be prevented from exercising it.* It is all the more intolerable since it is known that tens, perhaps hundreds, of thousands of them desperately *want* to come to Israel, and that nothing stands between them and the fulfillment of their dreams except the Soviet Government's ban. Every attempt to raise the question through the diplomatic channel has failed. The answer is unvarying: "This is interference in the domestic affairs of the Soviet Union," a breach of diplomatic etiquette. Formally, by its own concepts, the Soviet Government may be

---

* On March 9, 1949, the Knesset endorsed, as a "basic principle" of foreign policy, "assurance of the right of exit from every country to Jews who wish to return and make their home in their historic homeland." Mr. Ben Gurion, outlining his policy on October 7, 1951, said the Government would "look to the right of the Jews in all countries to emigrate to Israel and to share in the upbuilding of the Land." The present Government, which took office in 1955, varied the formula slightly, but not in essentials: "The Government of Israel will strengthen its ties with all countries which help to promote the security and development of Israel and enable their Jewish communities to share in the upbuilding of Israel and to emigrate to it." Mr. Ben Gurion quoted this "basic principle" in the Knesset debate on the Eisenhower Doctrine on June 3, 1957 (*cf.* pp. 158-159 above).

right. These Jews are Soviet citizens, bound by Soviet laws. But Israel feels for them the special affection that parents feel toward a handicapped child and has never been willing to accept the Soviet "no" as final. Practice in the smaller Communist countries has varied, ranging from Bulgaria, where for years all Jews were free to leave and nine out of every ten in fact left, to Czechoslovakia, where emigration is forbidden. A particularly cruel case is that of Rumania, where, after a period in which Jews were allowed to leave for Israel freely, a sudden ban was imposed. A quarter of a million Jews remain behind, many of them with wives and children already in Israel, tormented by their enforced separation.

Israel has never given up hope that one day things may change and that the Soviet Union will allow its Jews to come if they want to. As things are, they are tending to become pledges for Israel's good behavior. The Soviet Government assumes that Israel will never willingly do anything that might prejudice the prospects of Jewish emigration. Israel is nobody's satellite, but there is nothing like making sure; by allowing a tiny trickle of very old people to depart for Israel, the Soviet Government has been keeping the door of hope just perceptibly ajar.* Nothing else has thrown such a cloud over Israel-Soviet relations. Immigration is not only Israel's lifeblood, "the guarantee of her security and future," as Mr. Ben Gurion has said; it is her very essence, her soul. The sin against immigration is the one sin she cannot forgive. Israel's

---

* As late as mid-1957, when the Knesset discussed Israel's attitude to the Eisenhower Doctrine, members of left-wing *Government* parties were saying that "their main reason for not being able to support Israel's adherence to the Doctrine was that, by thus identifying itself with the U.S., the Government might prejudice the possibility that the U.S.S.R. might permit the emigration of Jews to Israel" (*Jerusalem Post,* June 4, 1957).

relations with Poland have improved beyond recognition since Jewish emigration was renewed in 1956. Her relations with the Soviet Union can never change basically as long as the ban persists.

10

The Foreign Service

Six weeks before the General Assembly's resolution of November 29, 1947, the Jewish national institutions in Palestine appointed a top-level committee to plan the administrative structure of the Jewish state. The committee set to work with a will. Almost its first step was to delegate subcommittees to blueprint the machinery of government, department by department.

It fell to me, as a one-man subcommittee, to plan the Foreign Ministry. I was at the time principal of the Jewish Agency's Public Service College and no more than guessed that I was to become the Ministry's director-general.

The Public Service College had been established in 1946

by a remarkable act of prescience on the part of the Jewish Agency's Political Department. The need had been felt for an institution which would train cadets for the Jewish public service, not necessarily for the Political Department alone. Out of nearly six hundred candidates, twenty-five, including five women, were selected by an examination whose novelty caused something of a stir in the country, though it was based on principles and methods tried, and shown sound, elsewhere. It was not long before press and public came to nickname the College "the school for diplomats." The students themselves probably felt by instinct that, whatever the declared purpose of their training, they were in fact fitting themselves to be Foreign Service officers of the Jewish state. Ironically, as the Jewish state came closer to realization, the College gradually dissolved. By the time Israel's independence was proclaimed, not a single student, not even a girl, remained. They had drifted off, one by one, into the defense forces—at a pace which increased with the mounting violence of Arab attack.

But in the first few weeks after November 29 most of the students were still in residence. They formed themselves into study groups and began to inquire, mainly from books, how the foreign ministries of other countries worked. The raw material they accumulated became the basis for an "Outline Plan for the Foreign Office and Foreign Service of the Jewish State," the first draft of which I was able to draw up and submit to the parent committee by January 9, 1948. A second, final draft was ready before the end of the month—and put away in a drawer against the day of Jewish independence.

The "outline plan" was based on the assumption that "we should not spend more money on a Foreign Office than is absolutely necessary," though it was appreciated that "even a Foreign Office and Foreign Service run on modest lines must cost a good deal of money." The Foreign "Office" (as it was called before it came into existence) was to be headed by a director-general, assisted by a secretary-general responsible for the administrative services, including personnel, finance, registry, communications and protocol. There were to be seven "geographic" divisions: for the Middle East, Europe, Eastern Europe, North America, Latin America, the British Empire and Asia and Africa. This arrangement has continued to the present day, apart from changes in nomenclature: "Europe" and "North America" have become "Western Europe" and "United States," while "British Empire," in keeping with the times, is now "Commonwealth." In addition, six "functional" divisions were provided for: United Nations, Consular, Economic, Legal, Information and Training and Research. These divisions, too, have remained substantially unchanged, except that "United Nations" has been broadened into "International Organizations," while "Training and Research" is now "Research" only.

The Political Department of the Jewish Agency, which had been a Foreign Ministry in all but name and external authority, was wound up with the establishment of Israel as a sovereign state. It had conducted a good deal of its written work in English, partly because it addressed itself in the main to the British Government and the British mandatory administration in Palestine, and partly because some of its representatives abroad were not familiar with Hebrew. This was now to change. The "outline plan" specified that "the language used in the Foreign Office, and for correspondence between the Foreign Office and Foreign Service establishments abroad, shall be Hebrew, subject to any special exigencies of the service." The Director-General was to "take an early opportunity of standardizing Hebrew equivalents for expressions current in diplomatic practice." These objects were duly carried out, though it is only fair to record that the task of "standardizing Hebrew equivalents" was accomplished, almost singlehanded, by the Foreign Minister himself. It was a labor of love and has enriched the Hebrew tongue.

The "outline plan" went on to stipulate that the diplomatic and consular services were to be regarded as a single service, to be called "the Foreign Service," whose personnel was to be interchangeable with that of the Foreign Office. The highest rank in the Foreign Service was to be "Minister in charge of a Legation (technically, Envoy Extraordinary and Minister Plenipotentiary)." The Jewish state was not to have ambassadors and embassies. These were thought to be too grand and expensive, and perhaps too invidiously distinctive, for a new state whose budget was likely to be as modest as its ambitions. What was thought good enough, at the time, by Swizerland and Finland would certainly be good enough for us.

As it happened, it was not long before Israel's first ambassador was appointed. Immediately after the elections of January 1949, the United States granted *de jure* recognition to the Government of Israel, which now replaced the old Provisional Government. The time had come to normalize American diplomatic representation. Early in February the United States made known its intention of raising its "Mission" in Israel to an embassy and appointing its "Special Representative" ambassador. The proposal came as a complete surprise and indeed caused some confusion, so remote was it from anything Israel had had in mind.* But the confusion lasted no more than a few minutes. It was realized at once that this was not an offer that could or should be refused, especially as at that time the United States was represented in several Arab states by ministers only. Soon afterward Israel established her own embassy

---

* Cf. the new ambassador's own account: James G. McDonald, *My Mission in Israel* (New York, Simon and Schuster, Inc., 1951), pp. 125–27.

in Washington, similarly raising her Special Representative to the rank and style of ambassador.

Today Israel has ambassadors at London, Paris, Moscow, Ottawa, Rome, Buenos Aires, Stockholm, Rangoon, The Hague, Berne and Accra and Monrovia as well as at Washington. With the old distinction between ambassadors and ministers disappearing rapidly, and sensibly, all over the world, and with even Finland and Switzerland following the general trend, it can be only a matter of time before Israel's heads of mission everywhere have ambassadorial rank.

This point, relatively trivial, is not the only one in which experience and practice have outstripped the "outline plan" of January 1948. The mechanics of the Foreign Ministry and Foreign Service have retained, in essence, the pattern laid down in the first draft, but their dynamics could not be foretold as precisely. The plan listed the diplomatic and consular posts which were to be opened soon after establishment of the Jewish state. It divided them, in terms of time, into three categories. Legations at London, Washington, Paris and Moscow and "Passport Control Offices" at Hamburg, Frankfurt, Vienna and Bucharest were to be set up "immediately"—the legations in view of the obvious importance of the four capitals, and the passport control offices, for the issue of visas, to meet the urgent needs of Jewish displaced persons and refugees. The second category, of posts to be opened "as soon as possible," included consulates-general at Shanghai (for the Far East), Prague (for Eastern and Southeastern Europe), Ankara and Teheran, a consulate at Warsaw, and passport control offices at Aden, Algiers and Trieste. Again, the needs of would-be immigrants were paramount: they dictated the pattern of consular representation in particular. Lastly, in the third group, posts which were to be established "before six months have passed," were consulates-general at Stockholm (for Scandinavia) and at Rio de Janeiro (for Latin America) and con-

sulates at Bombay, Brussels, Rome, Johannesburg, Montreal
and Melbourne. Here political considerations were beginning to come into their own: Israel was to be represented in
potentially friendly countries, with an eye, too, to the importance of Asia (Bombay), good-neighborliness in the Mediterranean (Rome), the voting strength of the Latin American
republics in the United Nations (Rio de Janeiro) and, not
least, some main centers of Jewish life (Johannesburg, Montreal, Melbourne). Curiously enough, New York, which was
to become the Foreign Ministry's biggest dependency abroad
and in fact had a consul-general appointed to it two days after
Israel achieved independence, was not mentioned in the "outline plan."

There were, in practice, considerable deviations from this
plan, even at the start. Consular or visa offices were opened at
Munich and Berlin instead of at Hamburg and Frankfurt,
handling heavy immigration traffic from and through Germany until, after a few years, when there was no longer need
for them, they were closed. The offices at Aden and Shanghai,
as well as another which operated at Salzburg from July 1948
to the end of 1949, were also closed as soon as they had seen
most of the immigrants on their way.

The "outline plan," which had provided that the Foreign
Service was to "be constituted in the first instance on as modest a scale as possible," recognized at the same time that its
expansion would have to "be carried on as rapidly as conditions
allow or demand." Israel, in fact, has world-wide interests and
needs which require diplomatic and consular representation
on a scale disproportionate to her size. The country's own geographic extent is no criterion. Surrounded as she is by enemies,
Israel looks for friends in every part of the world. The Arab
economic boycott compels her to seek economic ties outside
the Middle East, wherever she can. The constant preoccupa-
tion of the United Nations with problems affecting Israel

calls for political activity in every capital. The bonds of affinity and interdependence with the Jewish diaspora imply something like a universalization of Israel, and consequently of her Foreign Service. At the present time Israel is represented abroad by twelve ambassadors (accredited to twenty countries), fifteen ministers (accredited to twenty-nine countries), one "diplomatic representative," three chargés d'affaires and thirty-seven consuls-general and consuls (including honorary consuls). Her diplomatic and consular posts are manned by a total of 682 officials, of whom 427 are local employees. The staff of the Foreign Ministry in Jerusalem numbers 338; this includes everyone who works on the premises, night watchmen, office cleaners and all.

Nothing like this was envisaged, nor could have been, when the "outline plan" first sketched the pattern of Israel's representation abroad. Israel was not in existence; there could be no full awareness of the needs and opportunities that would arise in ten wonderful, tempestuous years.

In particular, the "outline plan" did not take into account the possibility—which soon became a likelihood and almost at once a certainty—that the timetable for building up the Foreign Ministry would be upset by physical causes. The aim was to have ready by May 15, 1948, "the nucleus of a working Foreign Office" and "the most essential Foreign Service officers at twenty-four hours' notice to leave." To achieve this, a director-general was to be appointed by February 1 and a secretary-general not more than ten days later. Between February 10 and March 15 the Foreign Office and Foreign Service were to be organized and the senior officers in both appointed. The second half of March was to see the "dispatch of representatives to negotiate recognition with foreign Governments." By May 15 seventy-two officials were to be at their desks in the new Ministry, and forty Foreign Service "personnel" ready to leave.

Actually, things turned out very differently. On May 15 only two officials started work with the Foreign Minister in Tel Aviv—the rest were caught in the siege of Jerusalem, unable to get away. The truce called by the Security Council came into force on June 11. The following night at nine I set out from Jerusalem in a jeep which carried, besides me, an army officer (who was later to become military attaché at Washington), the officer's wife (who had been one of the five girls at the Public Service College), a driver and an old German MG-34—in case word of the truce had not reached all the Arab troops who commanded the highway from the hills on either side. Part of the route lay along the new "Burma Road," roughed out of the secret hills a few nights before. One stretch of it could still not take a loaded jeep; for half a mile we walked. All Israel seemed to be on the move that night—hundreds of volunteers carrying supplies to Jerusalem on their backs, silhouetted black against the stars; silent soldiers heading east and west like a straggle of ants, guided seemingly by instinct; political leaders on their way down to join the Government at Tel Aviv, others going up to see how Jerusalem had fared in the siege. Old friends met unexpectedly in the rocky night, stopped just long enough to exchange a few words. In the end we reached Tel Aviv without much trouble at three in the morning. By eight, I had started work in the villa at Sarona which since May 28 had housed the Foreign Ministry. Not till a day or two later did I ask who was to be director-general. "Why, I thought you would be," said the Minister. One of my first tasks was to reply to a letter of congratulations which the only Jewish resident of Liberia had sent to the Prime Minister on the achievement of independence. Almost the next was to decide what was to be the adjective of Israel—Israelite, Israelian, or what? It was agreed, after a discussion in which everyone in the office took part, that a citizen of Israel would be an Israeli, while the adjective proper should be

Israel. (This has not quite stood the test of time nor been universally accepted. People speak of "the Israel army" or "Israel agriculture," but equally of "Israeli children" or "the Israeli plains.")

The organization of the Foreign Ministry was now taken in hand in earnest. A month later the original staff of two had grown to just over a hundred. There was no time to organize before starting work. Everything had to be done at once. The Security Council was in session at New York—the truce was to last only four weeks. It was essential to have Israel recognized by the largest possible number of other countries. The first diplomatic missions had to be established abroad. Some sort of budget had to be scraped together. Work was constantly interrupted by air-raid warnings; vital problems were discussed and decisions taken in the cellar. Many things were still wholly outside the experience of anyone on the staff. No one knew, for instance, how to draft letters of credence—with the result that when Israel's first minister presented himself at Prague, his letters were not accepted by the Czechoslovak Government.

The new Ministry was fortunate in being able to draw on the staff and experience of the Political Department of the Jewish Agency. The Department's officials made their way to Tel Aviv one by one, convoyed out of Jerusalem through the Arab Legion lines. They were all old friends who had mostly known one another and worked together for years. This eased the immediate problem of personnel, though the Foreign Ministry of an independent state naturally differed, in its procedures and objects, from the Political Department of a Jewish Agency which had spoken in the name of Jews all over the world. The staff had to adjust their thinking and methods accordingly. The Jewish Agency had made "submissions" to the British High Commissioner. This now belonged to the past, and the novel vocabulary of diplomacy had to be acquired. Since May 15 the Political Department's officials in Jerusalem had replied to the British consul-general's communications—all still addressed to the Jewish Agency—pointedly in the name of the Provisional Government of Israel. That hungry month between independence and the lifting of the siege had at least, for all its frustrations, accustomed them to thinking in the new terms which sovereignty implied.

There has never been any lack of applicants for posts in the Foreign Ministry and Foreign Service, but this does not mean that the problem of staffing has been easy. The intake from the Jewish Agency's Political Department was quickly exhausted—as soon as the Ministry began to overtake the Department in scope and size. Early recruitment was mainly by recommendation; a large number of people had to be found in a very short time. Unsatisfactory as this method was, it produced fewer misfits than might be supposed, and the Ministry has been able, in the course of years, to rid itself of many of these, despite the difficulties which attend dismissals (except for crime) in any civil service. Since 1953 entry into the senior, or "diplomatic," grades has been by examination only. The examination, generally held once a year, is open to university graduates between the ages of twenty-three and twenty-eight; exceptionally, an outstanding candidate may be admitted up to the age of thirty. This system has, so far, produced good results. Technical staff is engaged through the machinery of the Civil Service Commission and the labor exchanges. Although the Foreign Ministry is no more popular with press and public in Israel than foreign ministries are elsewhere in the world,* there is a constant stream of persons, qualified

---

* I should not wish to be misunderstood. Whatever press and public may think of the Foreign Ministry, foreign *affairs* are popular with both. There are few people in Israel who do not regard their country's external relations as a direct concern, or even responsibility, of their own. A few years ago three young men were walking along a street

and unqualified, who seek admission. It is generally supposed that it is the lure of foreign travel which attracts these many hundreds of aspirants, but probably no single explanation fits every case. It remains true that in a period when other ministries in Israel have encountered serious difficulties, partly because of low pay, in recruiting their staffs, the Foreign Ministry, where pay is no better, has never found itself thus embarrassed. Its embarrassment has been that of riches.

The general quality of the Foreign Ministry's staff has been high. Like the people of Israel as a whole, its members come from all over the world, though the proportion of native-born Israelis naturally rises each year. This diversity of origin and talent has brought difficulties in its train. Educated in Egypt, Chile, Britain, Poland, Italy, Argentine, the United States, Germany, South Africa and a dozen other countries, Foreign Ministry officials have been accustomed to think and express themselves in a variety of ways, which it has not always been easy to bring to a common denominator without its being the lowest. But diversity has also had its compensations. United in a common cause, citizens and servants now of a single state,

---

in Jerusalem, time heavy on their hands. They stopped by a house which looked easy to break into. Inside, there was a safe, which they contrived to open. In the safe they found more gold than was good for them. A few days later they were caught, but refused absolutely to say where they had hidden their haul. The police tried everything, promises, cajolery and threats; but to no effect. After a while, a woman social worker took one of the youngsters aside. She asked him if he knew what house it was they had broken into and discovered he had no idea. "Well," she told him, "you might as well know—it was the Netherlands legation. You know Israel doesn't have many friends in the world, and the Dutch are among the few real friends we have. It would be terrible if a thing like this spoiled our relations with them." "Heavens," said the lad, "we never guessed it was anything like that! Why didn't anyone tell us?"—and at once he explained where the gold was hidden.

members of the Foreign Ministry staff have enriched one another, and the Ministry itself, by the very variety of their
experience and outlook. It did not, in fact, take long before
they welded themselves into a team which could at least invite,
if not challenge, comparison with any likely to be found in
the Foreign Ministry of a small new state.

Party influences have from the start been strong in the Israel
civil service, but much less so in the Foreign Ministry than in
almost any other. The Minister for Foreign Affairs has,
throughout the past ten years, been a member of Mapai, the
Labor Party dominant in the Government coalition. But never
at any time has more than a handful of the Ministry's senior
officials belonged to this party, and even these attained the
positions they did on their merits; their party membership has
been coincidental and irrelevant to their work or standing as
civil servants. Every effort has, in truth, been made to keep the
Ministry free from party pressures or considerations, and there
have, to my knowledge, been two exceptions only. The first is
that of the Minister's own private political secretary. With the
Minister committed to much party business, the private secretary must be a member of his party and, as such, legitimately
privy to its counsels. The second exception relates to the heads
of diplomatic missions and raises wider questions of principle
and custom.

In some countries, such as Great Britain or France or Brazil,
all or almost all Foreign Ministry and Foreign Service posts,
from the highest to the lowest, are held by professional members of the diplomatic service who have made this their career.
When exceptions occur, it is only on grounds of exceptional
personal qualification for a difficult post at a difficult time. In
other countries, notably among the Latin American republics, the headship of a diplomatic mission is regarded as a re-
ward for distinguished political or public service; sometimes
it is a convenient way of removing to a distance an influential

national figure whose presence at home has become awkward. The ambassadors of such countries are rarely "career men"; they come from some other field of activity and return to it when their period of office is over. There is a third group of countries, of which the United States is the outstanding example, where the two systems are mixed—with some heads of missions "career men," and others "outsiders."

When Israel first organized her Foreign Service there were, of course, no "career men." The career itself had not existed, except in the shape of the Jewish Agency's political service; and it was from this service that Israel's first heads of missions were, in general, recruited. As time went on and the Foreign Service offered a new career, party pressures began to make themselves felt. Parties which at different times belonged to the Government coalition demanded that their men be taken into the Foreign Service, and in particular that they be appointed to top diplomatic posts. These demands became increasingly difficult to resist, because of the give-and-take between parties which coalition rule brings with it. But no head of mission has ever been appointed for his party loyalty alone. The Ministry has always insisted that candidates for such posts must have the needed qualifications and has reserved, and often exercised, the right to reject candidates put up by the parties if they did not meet its standards. At the present time not more than about one tenth of the heads of missions are party nominees, though the Foreign Service includes a fair number of other noncareer ambassadors and ministers chosen for their own special fitness for the posts they hold.

This system has worked, on the whole, without much friction. The reason for this lies perhaps in the fact that the distinction between politicians and officials is not as sharp in Israel as it is in some countries. It is fairly easy, and not unusual, for a man to move from one category into the other (and back again, if he wishes). Israel's first Foreign Minister himself became, as long ago as 1933, the political head of the Jewish Agency's Political Department, which until then he had served as its senior permanent official. Israel's present Ambassador to Ghana and Liberia was Minister to Czechoslovakia in 1948 and then Minister to Rumania. On returning home, he became Director-General of the Prime Minister's Office and later of the Ministry of Finance, before entering political life actively as a Mapai member of the Knesset. He resigned from the Knesset in 1957 to take up the post he holds now at Monrovia and Accra. It is, in general, no uncommon thing to find senior officials (but not officials of the Foreign Ministry) making speeches on party platforms. This blurring of the distinction between official and politician, whatever its disadvantages, is of respectable Zionist antiquity and has eased the Foreign Ministry's position when it has been necessary to appoint a political personage to an ambassadorial post. At the same time, the Ministry itself would not go out of its way to encourage the practice. Experience of the Ministry's workings is as important for an ambassador as for any member of his staff. If the "plums" of the service went regularly to persons from outside its ranks, career officers would be deprived of a vital incentive, and the number of really able applicants for entry into the service would almost certainly fall off. As things are, "outsiders" in top posts are too few to prejudice the morale of the service or damp the ardor of those who aspire to diplomacy as a career.

The Foreign Ministry has faced innumerable problems in staffing as in every other field, and it has by no means solved them all. One such problem is that of training. Pre-entry training has not proved feasible since the successful but short-lived experiment of the Public Service College. The Ministry has a full-time training officer who does what he can, not negligibly by any means, to conduct courses for the younger career officers as well as for technical and clerical staff. Members of the staff are encouraged to study at the university after office hours and in the evenings, and more than one has acquired a doctorate while in full employment with the Ministry. But pressure of work is the constant enemy of training and study, even for relatively junior officials. The Ministry as a whole is somewhat understaffed. This, as Lord Strang has pointed out,* may not in itself be a bad thing, but it makes it hard for anyone to do the concentrated reading which any form of study requires, or even be regular in attendance at a training course. New ways of training are constantly being tried and the Ministry's facilites extended. But ideal solutions still remain to be found, and the task is not made any easier by the fact that the nature of the problem keeps changing with the Ministry's development and needs.

A special problem is that of the employment of women in the Foreign Service. Like other countries, Israel admits women to government service equally with men in all respects, including pay. The Foreign Ministry has from the start accepted women and, at one early stage, even encouraged them. One woman served for years as chargé d'affaires at Montevideo, another was consul at New York even longer. It can be said truly that the women in Israel's Foreign Service have deserved well of their country; each has shown ability and distinction in her work. But quite apart from the problem of retirement on marriage and the consequent disruption of plans, familiar in the experience of every Foreign Service which employs women, more serious difficulties arise. A woman serving away from home tends to be afflicted by loneliness to a degree almost impossible to bear. This is true, certainly with Israeli girls, even of typists or registry clerks, who have greater opportuni-

---

* Lord Strang, *Home and Abroad* (London, André Deutsch, 1956), p. 282.

ties of finding congenial company (particularly where there is a large Jewish community or Israeli "colony") than women in more exalted positions. A woman at, or near, the head of a diplomatic mission can be happy only if she is very self-sufficient, content to confine herself to her work and official contacts. Normally a woman will find such a position intolerable and will become acutely unhappy, even if she should, by chance, never find herself actually embarrassed by reason of her being a woman. The first secretary of one of our embassies often, in her ambassador's absence, served as chargé d'affaires. Once, in this capacity, she had occasion to call officially on the ambassador of a Latin American republic, who was expecting the chargé d'affaires of Israel, but perhaps did not know she was a woman. As she came into the room, the ambassador blurted out: "Well, I must say, you're the most beautiful chargé d'affaires I've ever seen in my life!" The tribute was deserved, but the conversation was, to all intents, at an end.

There is no rule in the Foreign Ministry against sending women to responsible posts abroad. There could hardly be—when the Foreign Minister herself is a woman. If, in practice, women are now sent to such posts but rarely, it is for their own sakes. Experience has shown that it is only a very unusual woman who can be a diplomat and really happy.

Women do, however, play an important part in the Foreign Service—as their husbands' wives. Over and over again, in Israel's experience no less than in that of other countries, the success of a mission has owed as much to the diplomat's wife as to the diplomat himself. A man's posting to foreign service, or his appointment to a particular capital, may depend on the suitability of his wife. At all events, the principle operates negatively: an unsuitable wife may spoil her husband's chances or even, in extreme cases, his career. By and large, the wives of Israel's representatives abroad have done well. Apart from their duties as hostesses, which in many posts are a full-time responsibility, they are in constant demand for work in the Jewish community. Like their husbands, they have to guard against idolization. Jews abroad will be so fired with enthusiasm for Israel that they lionize those who represent her. It takes a strong or hardened character not to confound enthusiasm for Israel with admiration for one's own person. On the whole, Israel's representatives abroad have kept their balance and have emerged, not too battered, from what in some posts is a heady ordeal.

Many countries adopt the practice of appointing honorary consuls in towns, particularly ports, in which the volume of commercial or shipping business makes it useful to maintain consular representation but does not justify the employment of a full-time salaried career officer. These posts are coveted by local citizens, often for reasons of prestige and standing. Often, too, the honorary consul will have a legitimate personal interest in trade between his own country and the country he represents. Israel has been chary of making too many such appointments and has, all told, a little more than twenty honorary consuls, two thirds of them in Central and South America. These men have served Israel well, giving lavishly of their time and resources and receiving very little in return. The Foreign Ministry is frequently asked why it is so sparing with appointments of this kind. The question is asked most often by Ministry of Finance officials and members of the Knesset who cast around for likely economies and believe that in many posts career officers could well be replaced by unpaid local representatives.

It is, in fact, the Foreign Ministry's policy to avoid the appointment of honorary consuls as far as possible. In most cities there is a Jewish community which would take it as a reflection on itself if any person other than a Jew were ap-

pointed.* The choice, therefore, is limited in practice to leading members of the Jewish community, two or three of whom
will tend to regard themselves, and to be regarded by their
supporters, as most fitted for the honor. It becomes impossible
to appoint one without offending the others and, since Israel
has no desire to create local jealousies or dissensions, it is
usually best to appoint none. There is, too, a strong wish in
Jewish communities everywhere to see a "genuine" Israeli
represent Israel, and an equally strong realization on the part
of the Foreign Ministry that so complex and swiftly changing
a country as Israel must be represented, if it is to be represented effectively, by someone who knows it intimately from
within. Even if Jewish citizens of other countries can sometimes be convincing spokesmen for Israel, it is not fair, nor
always useful, to place them in this position vis-à-vis their local
authorities. If further justification were needed for the Ministry's policy, it would be found in the exceptionally heavy
burden which honorary consuls of Israel are called upon to
bear. Their duties are not confined to the occasional endorsement of a ship's papers, attendance at official functions, or prolongation of a passport for some Israeli citizen who may come
their way. In most places it is not long before they find themselves devoting the greater part of their time, willy-nilly, to
Israel's affairs. With interests in every field, Israel makes heavy
demands on those who represent her, and the duties of an
honorary consul soon cease to be purely honorific.

All members of the Foreign Service work under strain.
There is no such thing as an idle Israeli diplomat. No representative of Israel need ever ask himself what there is for him
to do next; there is always more than he can cope with. If the
Foreign Service had double the staff it has, it would still be

---

* Israel has, in fact, only one honorary consul who is not a Jew—at
Reykjavik, in Iceland, where there is no Jewish community.

more than fully extended. Six heads of missions have died during the relatively short time Israel has existed. Two died at home, a few weeks after resigning on grounds of health; four died suddenly of heart seizure at their posts. Not one of them was really old—they were in their early sixties at the most. It might be wise for Israel to enforce a rigid age limit at sixty, as other countries do. After sixty the strain of diplomatic life, certainly for a representative of Israel, grows too severe. There is too much to do, especially for men who never spare themselves in doing it. This chronic overwork is not the personal foible of a few; it is forced on all by Israel's exceptional needs and by their own sense of mission. Perhaps, as the years pass, the pace may slow down, but there seems no such prospect yet.

The Foreign Ministry's budget has never been really adequate to its needs—that is, to what it regards as the needs of the country. It received I£10,436,400 for the budgetary year 1956–57, and I£10,650,000 for 1957–58—that is, just under $6,000,-000. Authorization has been given, especially in recent years, for only limited expansion of diplomatic and consular representation, and for little in the way of increased services. Criticism is often made of the inadequacy of Israel's information activities abroad—and indeed at times when these activities have been most essential they have had to be performed on a shoestring. Foreign Service salaries have been steadily cut; they are now, as they have probably always been, the lowest in the world. Foreign Service establishments have been reduced too, with the result that in many posts one man, in practice, does work which should be done by two or three. The small annual increase in the budget has been due in the main to higher salaries at home, which have had to keep pace with the rise in the cost of living, and to a parallel rise in other expenses, such as postage and cable costs.

The charge is sometimes heard that the Foreign Ministry is only a spending department and that it does not, like the Ministry of Finance or the Post Office, produce income. The accusation, apart from being untrue, is unjust. Nowhere are foreign ministries, nor can they be, revenue-earning departments in the narrow sense of the term. It so happens, however, that the Foreign Ministry of Israel probably brings more money into the public chest than any other ministry, except the tax-collecting Ministry of Finance. No computation has ever been made of the value, in terms of money, of Israel's representatives abroad. They are constantly engaged in the campaigns for voluntary funds contributed by Jews all over the world, in popularizing Israel bond issues, in securing official loans (as from the American Export-Import Bank) and grants-in-aid, in negotiating commercial agreements and stimulating trade in general, and in a variety of other revenue-producing activities. If it were not for them, there would be a heavy slump in Israel's income.

Yet it is a fact that foreign ministries are not popular with ministries of finance in any country. Israel's Foreign Ministry has perhaps no more cause to complain than most others, though more is expected of it than of foreign ministries elsewhere. It appreciates, too, that other ministries in Israel, though not all, are compelled to operate on insufficient budgets. It has no choice but to make the best of a difficult situation. Its minister at Mexico City is accredited to eight countries all told, its ambassadors at Buenos Aires and at Stockholm each to three, its ambassador at Rangoon and minister at Lima each to four. Some of this accreditation must remain purely formal, since no individual, however dedicated or hard-working, can hope to cover so vast a field. A good many other ambassadors and ministers are accredited to two countries each (Belgium and Luxembourg, Australia and New Zealand, Japan and Thailand, Brazil and Venezuela, Ghana and Liberia) and find it hard to meet all their commitments. Israel, with her interests everywhere, must strive for the widest possible diplomatic representation—but the task of making bricks without straw has not become any easier since her people first tried it three thousand four hundred years ago.

When the "outline plan" was drafted in the first days of 1948 there was little experience to go on. In the decade which has passed since then, the Foreign Ministry has learned a good deal—and has become conscious of how much more it has to learn. Many things, including some of the most important, cannot be learned at all by the present generation of senior officials. A French or British ambassador knows what it is to be a second secretary, a first secretary and a counselor: he has been them all himself. No ambassador of Israel has ever been less than a minister; and the functions of a minister do not differ from those of an ambassador except in name. There are now three or four ministers who have been first secretaries or counselors. This means that experience is being gained as time passes, but it must be ten or twelve years more before anyone who started as a second secretary is likely to become an ambassador. Generally speaking, promotion in the Foreign Service is rapid, partly because the number of posts to be manned has grown faster than the available staff, and partly because most junior officers tend to be young men in a hurry who do their utmost to get on. (They are appalled and incredulous when told that a former British ambassador to Israel spent the first fifteen years of his career in the rank of vice-consul. In a country with only ten years of independence behind it, fifteen years is a span of time which people find hard to conceive at all—and harder still to relate to themselves and their careers. It is doubtful whether young men would enter the Foreign Service if they thought they might remain vice-consuls for fifteen years or ten or even five—even though they knew that by ability and hard work they had every chance of becoming ambassadors in due time.)

The experience of ten years has, however, taught the Foreign Ministry a good deal. It now knows the special difficulties which a man encounters in his *second* post as head of mission—and can make him aware of them in advance. It has become clear that the grading of Foreign Ministry personnel will have to be revised, though this will not easily be accomplished; a civil service as egalitarian as the society it serves does not lightly permit deviations from the norm. Much has been learned about the rotation of officials between posts at home and abroad, and between one post abroad and another. Foreign Service officers tend to lose touch rapidly with the changing realities of Israel; a spell of duty at home every three or four years becomes essential if they are to represent their country effectively abroad.

The task of building up the Foreign Ministry and Foreign Service of Israel has been as satisfying and as engrossing as anyone could desire or conceive. It has been mostly light, with little shade. It has meant a great deal of hard work—but who would not wish to have worked hard these ten historic years? Service in the cause of Israel has rewards all its own: there have been few days which have not brought something in the way of excitement, romance or achievement.

Early in 1950 the minister of Israel to the Argentine Republic was given accreditation to Chile as well. In May he set out for Santiago to present his letters of credence. After the ceremony he began the usual round of formal calls on his new colleagues, the heads of the other diplomatic missions. In due course he came to the British ambassador, Sir Cecil Bertrand Jerram. To his surprise, the ambassador all of a sudden started humming the tune of *Hatikvah,* the national anthem of Israel.

In reply to the obvious question, the ambassador, then on the eve of retirement, told how in 1917, early in his career, he had been a young vice-consul at Odessa. One day a large concourse of Jews appeared outside the consulate—a demonstration of gratitude for the Balfour Declaration, by which the British Government, on November 2 of that year, had promised the Jewish people a national home in Palestine. The Jews had sung that song—with such force and fervor that he had remembered the tune ever since. Now, a third of a century later, at the other end of the world, he was welcoming as a colleague the minister of Israel—of that free and sovereign state for which the Jews of Odessa had yearned.

One evening in August 1957, in Jerusalem, I told this story at a farewell party for some colleagues leaving shortly for posts abroad. I told it to illustrate the compensations of service away from home. As I finished, one of the guests said quietly: "I was in that crowd!" And another: "So was I! It was on November 19. There were thirty thousand of us!"

I do not believe that the Foreign Service of any other country can offer the deep fulfillments which come of serving Israel. The fulfillments of service at home are deeper still.

Index

229

J

About the Author

WALTER EYTAN has been Director-General of the Ministry for Foreign Affairs of Israel from the first and, in fact, the author of the original blueprint for the establishment of this government department. He is forty-seven years old, and was educated in England at St. Paul's School, London, and Queen's College, Oxford. From 1934 to 1946 he was lecturer on German Philology at Oxford, and from 1946 to 1948 he was principal of the Jewish Agency's Public Service College in Jerusalem. He was head of the Israeli delegation at the armistice negotiations at Rhodes in 1949, at the Lausanne Conference later in the same year and at the "Atoms for Peace" Conference at Geneva in 1955.